D1535247

Nine
Poisons,
Nine
Medicines,
Nine
Fruits

Shambhavi Sarasvati

Jaya Kula Press
110 Marginal Way, #196
Portland, Maine 04101
jayakula.org

Cover and interior design and layout: *Libby Connolly*
www.libbyconnolly.com

Library of Congress Control Number: 2017912866

Sarasvati, Shambhavi
Nine Poisons, Nine Medicines, Nine Fruits

ISBN:
978-0-9841634-8-9
0-9841634-8-4

Printed in the United States of America on acid-free paper.

Nine
Poisons,
Nine
Medicines,
Nine
Fruits

Shambhavi Sarasvati

For Liu Ming, until we meet again

Various obstacles are the sign of spiritual accomplishment.
Without obstacles, there is no spiritual accomplishment.
If obstacles are recognized, they are spiritual accomplishments;
And if unrecognized, are obstacles indeed.[1]

—Longchenpa

CONTENTS

This text was compiled and revised from a series of dharma talks given by Shambhavi Sarasvati from December 2015 to April 2016 in Portland, Maine.

———

INTRODUCTION

The nine poisons are habits of body, emotions, and mind that distract or delay you from discovering who you really are. These repeating patterns—such as responding in predictable, habitual ways emotionally, or being enslaved to rigid, limited concepts of yourself and others—represent the loss of presence and immediacy. Instead of seeing clearly how things actually are and responding to *that*, your responses are conditioned, repetitive, and stale.

Conditioned habits of body, emotions, and mind lead you to become more entangled in complex, heavy situations. You make unskillful decisions. You are too passive or too aggressive. You partially, or completely, misinterpret circumstances. Your timing is off. Such habits are experienced in degrees of compulsion. Some are easy to change, others are not. You may become conscious of the momentum enjoyed by your conditioned habits only when you try to change them. When the momentum of habit meets the energy you deploy to redirect habit, you experience resistance.

Conditioned patterns always represent a quantity of fantasy projection that is unrelated to our real situation. We may be aware of the conditioning that drives our habitual perceptions, ideas, and emotional patterns, or we may be entirely unconscious of it. A counter-activity, such as meditation, eventually brings all of our conditioning to light. Many kinds of life experiences make us more aware of our conditioning. Ultimately, we realize that karmic habit patterns prevent us from freely expressing ourselves and participating fully in life.

The nine medicines are the remedies that help us to recover from limiting patterns. These remedies are built into our alive, aware reality and naturally arise to benefit us in the course of our lives. One of the most effective remedies is repeatedly not getting what we want. Sooner or later, this causes us to examine our approaches and to seek out new ones, including by seeking spiritual teachings.

The nine fruits are wisdom virtues that naturally appear on their own once obscuring conditioning is dissolved. Spiritual practices, such as meditation and mantra, help to relax conditioning. When our habitual patterning unwinds, we feel more integrated into life and less separate. An experience of freshness and immediacy arises. We discover greater freedom of self-expression, greater spontaneity, and more precision and skill in our ways of responding and relating and, ultimately, a profoundly uncontrived naturalness.

Teachings that speak about fundamental obstacles to waking up and discovering our real nature are a kind of genre, particularly in Buddhist traditions.[2] But none of the texts that I have read are all that specific to contemporary life, particularly life in the United States. Of course, they *do* apply to human beings in general. They are not in any way obsolete. But my experience working with myself and students is that we have some specific obstacles in the U.S. that deserve special attention. In this book, you will find that I place somewhat more emphasis on the obstacles of pride and intellectualizing, and on the limiting effects of the psychological View of the person.

In the great Indian epic, *The Mahabharata*,[3] pride always initiates the careening of circumstances away from unity and wisdom and toward entanglement and obstruction. Pride has always taken pride of place when it comes to making a mess of things. Here in the u.s., we have built an entire way of life based on pride and the self-defensiveness, self-promotion, insecurity, aggression, and struggle that are the hallmarks of a life lived in enslavement to pride.

We have also, to varying degrees, lost touch with the wisdom and immediacy of our senses. Many students of mine experience an impaired capacity to receive and rely on direct experience. Some of us are so over-reliant on thinking as our main way of relating to life, our most direct experience is actually of our thoughts and not of the life we are thinking about. The over-reliance on intellect is a great impediment to enjoying the fruits of spiritual practices such as meditation.

A third obstacle is the psychological View of the human being and the ways in which many people are embodying this View in their habitual responses to life. The psychological View, first promoted in the late 19th and early 20th centuries by Sigmund Freud, has maintained several stable, fundamental assumptions despite the critiques of classical Freudianism and partial movements away from his methods and biases.

The first of these assumptions is that a human being can be damaged in an essential way. This belief has given rise to a hugely robust discourse about trauma and deep attachments to narratives of trauma by actual people. The experience of trauma is real, but the many ways in which we solidify identities around narratives of trauma are historically and culturally conditioned. On the other hand, the View of both Trika Shaivism and Dzogchen is that we all possess *vajra* or adamantine nature. Although we often experience pain and suffering, our real nature cannot be damaged, or even affected, by circumstances arising in impermanence. Through doing spiritual practices, we can discover our real nature and encounter our original wisdom, virtue, and goodness. This is true for all people no matter what traumas have been encountered during life.

The second assumption of the psychological View is that a relatively complete explanation of a person is possible. Freud's *only* method was explanation. From his patients, Freud elicited narratives of childhood, of other important life events, and of dreams. He then explained each element of a patient's story with special reference to traumatic experiences and his proprietary narrative of the structure of a person's psyche: the id, the ego, and the superego. Freud's use of explanation amounted to a defining commentary that supplanted the original narrative produced by a patient.[4]

This method is only barely plausible if you limit the explanatory field to an extremely small number of factors and assume that a child is born with little to no conditioning. This is what Freud did in fact assume. For him, children were nearly blank slates when born, ripe for being "written on" by family circumstances. Yet, even if we don't refer to the idea of karma, the field of epigenetics has confirmed what every mother, and every yogi, already knows: human beings are born with innumerable strands of conditioning and experience already built in from birth. You can never completely explain a person or even a single experience. People are infinite events.

Despite this, Freud has bequeathed to us a near maniacal attachment to explanation as a mode of self-exploration, self-presentation, and relating. We are fixated on understanding ourselves, and on being understood, through a collection of narratives. Why are we the way we are, and why do we feel the way we feel? We spend our lives anxiously mining our immediate past, trying to figure out this "why" as if the answers would provide refuge from impermanence. We want everyone to understand us the way we understand ourselves. We become upset when other people don't accept our carefully crafted narratives. And these days, we shop our brand story around on social media, creating increasingly selective and promotional narratives of self through words and images.

The third assumption of the psychological View inherited from Freud is that by articulating and explaining circumstances, or by rewriting our stories, we can be relieved of the effects of those circumstances on our bodies, emotions, and minds. We can confirm that this continues to be a foundational assumption by looking at Freud's method and how it is still used to a large degree in "talk therapy." But we can also look at ourselves and the degree to which we depend on self-explanation, talking things out, and mutual understanding for our sense of well-being and self-worth. Specific trends, such as the reframing of victims as survivors and the deployment of aphorisms to transform negative thoughts and feelings, also derive from the semi-conscious View that explaining and rewriting are effective vehicles for deep transformation.

In contrast, both Trika Shaivism and Dzogchen work to help us to *divest ourselves* of a congealed story or fixed self-image. The kinds of polished up stories about ourselves that psychology begets may make us feel better, which may in some circumstances be welcome. But these more habitable stories still represent a high degree of conditioning. Our goal as practitioners is to live in a radically unconditioned state where past, present, and future are only functional reference points and not the bars of a prison. The remedy for suffering is not an explanation of suffering.

A Note About Reality and Its Names

The whatever-it-is for which we are all searching has many names. Twenty years ago, I would have felt uncomfortable calling it God. Now I'm happy calling it God or Lord. In the tradition of Trika Shaivism, God and reality are one and the same. A single, continuous, self-aware consciousness and its energy are the ground from which everything arises and of which everything is composed. This primordial, creative intelligence is synonymous with wisdom virtues such as compassion, clarity, and creativity.

In this book, I use these terms interchangeably: God, reality, the Supreme Self, essence nature, enlightened essence nature, aware livingness, alive awareness, presence, unconditioned presence, consciousness and energy, existence, Shiva Nature, the natural state, and I'm sure a few more I can't remember. Anandamayi Ma, my root teacher, simply called it *that*.

How To Read This Book

You can read this book straight through from cover to cover. You can also read whatever attracts you in whatever order it does. You might want to consider that Poison One relates to Medicine One and Fruit One. So another way of reading would be to read the ones, twos, and threes sequentially. However you choose to read, or however much, I hope it is of benefit.

Introduction

About Anandamayi Ma

Anandamayi Ma was a 20th-century avatar: a direct emanation of wisdom, born totally awake. While accounts of her enlightened activities are legion, she lived as a householder in unusually close contact with her devotees, advising them about all aspects of life, laughing with them, comforting them, singing, and simply allowing all those who came to find refuge in her presence.

Ma's teachings are precise, playful, gutsy, down-to-earth, inspiring, and deeply moving. She had little formal education, but her facility with language was breathtaking. She loved wordplay and could convey the subtlest teachings to tens of thousands of followers from all walks of life. A respected Varanasi Pandit, when asked in 1936 if Ma had Shastric authority to bestow the Gayatri mantra on female students, declared: "Ma's will is scriptural. No other opinion is necessary."[5] Ma is the guiding light of my life. She is often quoted in this book.

View

View is a special word in Indian and Tibetan spiritual traditions. View teachings give us the largest context for our spiritual practice and our lives. View teachings answer questions about what realized people have come to understand about the nature of reality, the nature of a human being, the process of cosmology, and of waking up. When we understand View, then we are less likely to get stuck in our practice or to overvalue the relative concepts and patterns of body, energy, and mind that make up our more limited, everyday experience.

View also means to recognize, to see. View is not something we just learn intellectually. We receive the View; we practice with the View; and we come to recognize and embody the View. When you see the word "View" capitalized in this book, I am speaking of this.

Once you have the View, although the delusory perceptions of samsara may arise in your mind, you will be like the sky; when a rainbow appears in front of it, it's not particularly flattered, and when the clouds appear it's not particularly disappointed either. There is a deep sense of contentment. You chuckle from inside as you see the facade of samsara and nirvana; the View will keep you constantly amused, with a little inner smile bubbling away all the time.[6]

—Dilgo Khyentse Rinpoche

Introduction

POISONS

POISON ONE

Self-concern at the expense of others

One morning I got up and went into the kitchen. A student was eating breakfast at the table. Earlier, she had started to fill our water dispenser with filtered water, but she had abandoned it mid-project. The dispenser was sitting mostly empty, tucked away at one end of the counter.

"What happened to the water?" I asked her.

She answered, "I forgot about it. I got distracted."

"What did you forget about?"

"I forgot about filling the water bottle."

"No, that's not what you forgot about! This is a trick question."

We both laughed, she a bit nervously.

After pondering for a moment, my student was still stumped. What had she forgotten? She couldn't come up with anything other than forgetting to fill the container.

"You forgot that other people might need water," I said.

We forget about other people because we are distracted by

self-concern. Being overly concerned with our own inner machinations or narrow desires, whatever they may be, takes up much of our day. When we are in this state, the real circumstances of other people disappear. Our connection to the wisdom of the heart is blocked. We lose contact with natural reciprocity, with natural play. We call this numbness ordinary life.

Karma is another way of talking about self-concern. Karma consists of repeating patterns of consciousness and energy moving through time. We experience karma as compulsive, habitual reactions of body, emotions, and mind in the forms of pleasure, comfort-seeking, fear, anxiety, jealousy, competitiveness, sadness, and anger. Karmic conditioning is difficult to relax because these patterns have tangible energy and momentum. We experience this momentum directly when we try to change a habit. As our intention to change meets the momentum of the old habit, an experience we call "resistance" arises.

Karma magnetizes or collects around the conviction that there is actually something here to defend. You feel compelled to defend yourself against criticism. You feel compelled to defend your-self against being rejected. You must aggressively try to achieve reassuring outcomes. You must defend against even a moment of unsatisfied desire.

When we are distracted by the hodgepodge of patterns of body, emotion, and mind that we call our self, our vision is extremely selective and narrow. It's like having glaucoma or blind spots—big chunks of other people go away. Big chunks of our experience and perception go away. Our ability to feel the energy of any situation is radically diminished. Our ordinary condition of self-concern is a condensed, dense state. We are looking out for me, myself, and I.

My student's response to being questioned about what she had forgotten is an ordinary mind response. You are here, the water dispenser is here, your breakfast is here, and that's all you see. You don't see the other people coming down for breakfast a little later on.

"What did you forget? I forgot to fill the water bottle." It seems so reasonable. Most of us wouldn't think anything other than oh yes, of course, that's what I forgot.

We live with five people. So one person is eating breakfast while the nearly empty water dispenser sits off to the side somewhere, not available for anybody to use, and there are four other people in the house. Four people are invisible; they are gone. What you are actually forgetting is the whole rest of the world.

Self-concern results from the erroneous idea that we are just this little body harboring a kernel of awareness hurtling through space. When this ephemeral and fragile self is mistaken for the totality of what we are, then we have worries! Our experience of separation from life gives rise to anxious self-concern, defensiveness, and aggression. This sense of separateness is our root karma, our root distraction.

The separative self comes up with all kinds of subtle and not-so-subtle expressions of its drive to continually reassure itself and establish a ground. When you are in that condition, you are inevitably going to be, at least in part, not actually caring for anybody else. You are always going to perceive the world as threatening in some way, as difficult in some way. Struggle will be at the center of your experience. This is not a very nourishing circumstance.

Self-concern also creates a situation of lack of joy. When you are having the experience of anxious self-concern, it becomes difficult to connect with the joy of exchange with other people, of being immersed in that vast mix of communication. You cannot fully connect to the joy of being generous, of generously overflowing. Many, many exchanges between you and others that could be a source of enjoyment actually feel exhausting because you are always defending and aggressing.

Anxious self-concern is a noose around your neck. You are gasping for air. It's a situation of radical lack of nourishment. Real nourishment comes from feeling the communicative energy of your circumstance and being able to freely express yourself. You can give and receive with no other motive other than the joy of doing that. Self-concern leaves you with a very small View, a very small circle of experience, a very small set of concerns, and that's really what we are trying to leave behind when we do spiritual practice.

For instance, if my motivation for teaching was to prove something, or to get admiration, I would feel as if I were trying to move a wall pressed right up against my nose. Everybody else would be missing. All of you would be missing. The freshness and joy would be missing. Only this stale little self and its struggle to assert itself would be present to me. You all would appear only as monochromatic players in my little drama.

Self-concern always ends up being cruel. You can't help but be cruel, because you're going to manipulate the hell out of everybody else trying to satisfy a nervous little bundle of karmas. You're going to be very strategic in your relationships with other people. You're going to try to force people and situations to give you what you want. You're going to compete with other people and try to prove that you're better. You're going to take things away from other people deliberately because you think you need what others have. You're going to treat other people as less valuable than the demands of your karma. You're just going to do these things as a matter of course, as a matter of ordinary, daily life. Your daily life is going to be filled with consciously or unconsciously perpetrated violence.

When you express self-concern at the expense of other people, you are announcing that you don't fully understand the value of life, that you really are not in contact with the primordial beauty of everything, that you are not really in contact with life's continuity. Undue self-concern is just a big, blaring announcement that you actually have not yet recognized the fundamental reality to any large degree—because once you do, that self-concern is radically undermined. It begins to naturally liberate.

Overweening self-concern is still concern; it's still caring. It's enlightened caring under tension, under pressure. The same concern operates continuously and unbrokenly at all levels, contracted or expanded. When we start to wake up, that caring becomes liberated. When it expands, it becomes that joyful expression of caring for everyone and every aspect of the creation. When it contracts, it is self-concern at the expense of others. So no matter what condition you are in now, you do have the capacity for caring, for compassion, built right into your tensions.

We always say in Tantra, "as above, so below." Everything in our ordinary experience is made by and of a continuous, totally awake consciousness and its creative power. The overweening, limited, suffocating, cruel, non-nourished, strangulated, condensed, dense, anxious, fearful, angry, jealous, competitive self-concern that we experience is actually *that* infinite, pervasive Self showing up as us.

Your small self expresses the unlimited wisdom of Self as if it has been packed into a garbage compactor and squished. So your self-concern is not something that you need to attack or eject. It's something that you need to liberate so that you can discover more of the joy of caring for and giving to other people, so you can look outward and rediscover your passion for exploring the creation.

Here in the u.s., we are caught up in a particular flavor of self-anxiety that has to do with how much we achieve in life. It's rooted in the competitiveness of our society. We approach everything as some sort of contest. It's crazy how we live with such a competitive orientation. That competitiveness lends density and heat and cruelty to the ways in which we relate to ourselves and others. We think that there is so much at stake in how we appear to other people and how successful we are. We are measuring ourselves all the time. Other cultures in the world have that burden too, but it isn't universal.

We start off practicing in our spiritual traditions with a large measure of limited and limiting self-concern. That is our real condition for the most part. In our psychologized cultures, our gaze is

27

Poison One

often inward and distressed. This is a heavy condition to be in. How can we take our self-concern out for a walk and bring it into a larger arena? How can self-concern be freed to become selves-concern? That's where spiritual practice can help us.

On the other hand, a certain amount of heavy inwardness comes with the territory for people who are interested in spiritual growth. A measure of earnest self-concern flavors our earlier movements toward liberation. We worry ourselves with questions such as, "Will I ever be free?" Self-concern can even increase when we more fully recognize our limitations. This kind of self-concern can motivate practice. We need to have some of that; otherwise, we would never get started.

Initially, our motivation might be to achieve some definite, pre-defined idea of liberation, or to get some powers, or even just to feel better, or to make the teacher admire us. But if you are lucky, these motivations will not last long. The only motivation that will free you from the prison of self-concern is the desire to participate to your utmost in the vast carnival of life. You have to desperately want to know your real nature. From my experience, this is the only motivation that actually causes you to 100 percent want to drop your karmas. Any other motivations, even grand-sounding motivations such as achieving a light body, are halfway there. You are still determined to hold onto concepts and projections.

At some point, you realize that this is the world you are in and that you don't know very much about it. How deeply and subtly and skillfully can you participate? You get to the point where you don't want to be looking at this vast landscape from behind the bars of a tiny little cage, even the cage of spiritual concepts.

If your primary motivation is to fix yourself because you feel badly about things, well, that'll get you part of the way. If your motivation is to beat out the competition, that'll get you part of the way. If your motivation is to prove something about yourself, that'll get you part of the way. But eventually, you will trip up on that kind of self-concerned motivation. The process will eventually start to resist small self, and you will hit a wall. You will get turned back over and over again until you are ready to walk the path in a softer, more modest and open-ended way.

POISON TWO

Self-neglect at the expense of the capacity to realize

When we talk about self-neglect, we want to remember that in some spiritual traditions, self-neglect is considered to be a form of spiritual practice. Religiously-sanctioned forms of self-neglect include not eating enough, not sleeping enough, not bathing, not wearing clean clothes, not living in a habitable house, living outside, being impoverished, chastising desire through corporeal punishment, or otherwise neglecting your body.

Renunciates are people following various spiritual traditions who often practice self-abnegation. Some renunciates, or their traditions, believe that the measure of how much you care about others is demonstrated by the degree to which you neglect yourself. At the same time that they are neglecting themselves, many renunciates spend their lives providing service to others. Renunciation is an area of confusion for a lot of people, not just people in spiritual traditions.

Even ordinary people can have the idea that helping other people is morally superior to taking care of yourself. A lot of people harbor a subtle concept that self-abnegation is the only way to be of service and become or remain pure. Even if we are not part of a tradition that holds renunciation in high regard, simply being a citizen in a largely Christian culture can cause us to unconsciously absorb these assumptions.

Anyone who has worked in social services knows that helping others while ignoring your basic needs isn't a successful recipe. You must take care of yourself, or you eventually become useless to others. You slowly slip into exhaustion, confusion, anger, illness, and depression. This has happened to countless ordinary people, to people in spiritual traditions, and even to great religious renunciates such as Mother Theresa.[7] Most people find it impossible to maintain the clarity and energy required to help other people if they aren't taking care of themselves.

Those traditions that practice self-abnegation are called transcendental traditions. They have a basic attitude that matter and spirit are fundamentally different. Matter is the locus of sin, ignorance, suffering, and unwanted desires. Spirit is holy and pure. The focus is on detaching from material life, or at least the desires and needs of human bodies. Adherents may yearn for a kind of purification that leads to a different, less material form of embodiment.

In some Christian and Hindu traditions, transcendentalism is a core attitude. Many contemporary images we have of renunciates come from these two traditions, but especially from India. You have probably seen pictures of sadhus who spend a lifetime with withered arms raised to the sky and others who practice extremes of sexual sublimation and physical deprivation. For the average adherent, transcendentalism may be subtly and thoroughly woven into the culture of a tradition, and so it may not be explicitly articulated. But, for instance, the deeply rooted oppression of women and anxiety about sexuality that characterizes everyday Indian culture is in part a product of such transcendental views.

The direct realization traditions, such as Dzogchen and Trika Shaivism, hold the View that your body is actually your best vehicle for self-realization. They recognize that having been born with a human body is a beneficial situation. You can do a lot of different kinds of *sadhana* (spiritual practice) in a human body. You can meditate and do mantra. You can do kriya yoga and asana. You can study Ayurveda, you can dance, you can perform rituals, and you can sing.

Beings with other kinds of bodies may have deeper skills in one direction. For instance, they may see more clearly than we do, or they may run faster. Whales may be smarter than humans, but they can't pick up a lamp and light incense. Humans are considered to be the Jacks and Jills of all trades in the spiritual realm, and that's considered to be an opportunity.

The other potential advantage is that our senses are balanced. We have the same line-up of senses as other sentient beings, but other sentient beings tend to have one or two senses that are much stronger than the others. Humans senses are all just okay, but all okay works well for doing a variety of spiritual practices. In effect, the human realm is the sadhana realm. It's the realm in which you can come and do a lot of different kinds of practice, and so you have a lot of different opportunities to realize. That's why it's considered to be good to be born a human being.

Those of you who have studied purification practices such as *bhuta shuddhi* and *tattva shuddhi*, know that when we're doing those practices, we're taking a journey back to unconditioned consciousness and energy. But we're not getting in a rocket ship. We don't have to die and go to heaven. We don't even have to climb to a desolate mountaintop. We make this journey using our own bodies, energy, and minds. We're able to reenact cosmological processes in our own bodies, discover how reality works, and free ourselves from limiting patterns.

The ancient Tantras are View and practice manuals, many of which were written by Gurus for the benefit of their own students.

33

Poison Two

These texts emphatically state that we should take care of our bodies. We should treat our bodies honorably. We should try to be healthy so that we are not blocked or obstructed by illness from doing practice. The Tantras speak of our senses, and how we can use our senses to help us to realize and to explore our world. They discuss how our bodies are a microcosm of the macrocosmic process, and how we can discover everything by working with our own bodies.

> *Obtaining a superior birth and bestowed with a beautiful set of motor and sensory organs one who does not understand the best of his interests is like one who is self-slayer...Village, land, money, and house, could all be obtained again and again; but the human body could not be obtained over and again...wMen should make persistent efforts for the preservation of their bodies. It is not proper to let the body end itself by afflictions of disease like leprosy, etc.*[8]

The ancient Tantras also teach us that we have no need to go on external pilgrimages; the greatest pilgrimage is the human body. If you've done *kriya yoga*, you might have a sense of what this means. The different systems of kriya yoga teach you to engage with the natural activities taking place in your subtle channels and other structures of the subtle energy body. The simple kriya of breathing naturally and noticing the *sandhi*, or gap, at the beginning and end of each breath is a beautiful example of how the opportunity to practice is built in from the beginning. You discover that you already possess the means to wake up using your body, your breath, and your mind. You don't have to go elsewhere to find "it."

Anandamayi Ma often gave advice about taking care of our bodies. She said: "You have no right to inflict suffering on the body. Why not? Because everything belongs to God. God resides in the body."[9] She also gave advice for when you get sick. "If you are ill, go and consult the very best doctor. If you put yourself into the hands of the greatest, you may then remain free from worry and feel: 'Whatever happens is all right, I have done my utmost.' "[10] Our bodies are given to us to help us to realize; they're our instruments for realization. If we take care of them to the best of our ability, we are supporting our spiritual life.

In fact, Ma created circumstances that encouraged her devotees to tend lovingly to *her* body. People bathed her, fed her, dressed her, and led her around like a little child who had to be cared for in every way possible. In my View, Ma encouraged her devotees to relate to her like this so that we would learn how to care for ourselves and other people.

Self-neglect at the expense of our capacity to realize means that we don't pay enough attention to our physical health. We don't get enough exercise or proper movement practice. We don't eat correctly. We don't take proper care of ourselves when we're sick. We may lead erratic lives so that we're creating a lot of excess wind in our bodies, energy, and minds.

All of those *adharmic* activities cause imbalances of the five elements in our body. When we are out of balance, physical and mental distractions disturb our meditation. Our motivation and clarity may diminish. We may even stop practicing altogether. These symptoms of imbalance cause us to waste time and lose spiritual opportunities because we don't notice opportunities or cannot respond fully to them.

Of course, we are always going to have imbalances. Nobody can ever be in perfect balance, but every single one of us could do a better job of tending to our health. If you have studied a naturopathic wisdom tradition such as Ayurveda, you probably know a little about your constitution, what's good for you, and what's not good for you. Yet any number of times a week, most of us, myself included, don't adhere to those guidelines. Every time we ignore the wisdom of our health traditions, we are practicing self-neglect at the expense of our capacity to realize.

The real-life effects of self-neglect on our ability to do practice and wake up are physical discomforts that distract us; an

35

Poison Two

intensification of mental karmas, such as angry or fearful thought patterns; mental confusion; chronic sleepiness; sensory impairment; and stagnation generally. Any of these conditions will obstruct our sadhana. Attending to them through adjusting our diets and daily routines will go a long way toward creating more opportunity for us to wake up.

But supporting our practice is not just about taking care of our physical bodies. We also need to build lives for ourselves that encourage the relaxation of tensions. We all have different karmas. Some people are going to be in difficult, seemingly intractable circumstances. There is no blame attached to any kind of karma. But if we have the ability and circumstances to create a different kind of a life, we should do that! Having decent places to live, not being worried about where the next dollar is coming from, and not overworking all create good conditions for waking up. We have more time, more energy and more internal space for sadhana.

We also want to look at our relationships. We want to deliberately choose to be in relationships that support our values and are nourishing, or at least are not largely draining. Some people try to maintain relationships in which their partners are telling them, "Don't practice. Spend more time with me. Pay more attention to me. Follow the routine that feels more comfortable for me. Be more normal." Staying in such relationships is a form of self-neglect on your part. You want to be moving toward being in relationships in which people are supporting you to wake up, not trying to hinder you.

Many people have situations in which a partner is somewhat supportive. Your partner okay with you doing "some" practice, but please don't do it too much, or please don't do it when I want you to do something else. If what you want to do is practice, or what you want to do is come to satsang, or what you want to do is anything related to your spiritual life, then you don't want to be with a partner who tries to tug you in a different direction, even some of the time. We can make compromises about a lot of things. You want Chinese food, and your friend wants Indian food. Fine. You want to go to a ball game, and your friend wants to go to the arboretum. Fine. But why should you compromise your desire to self-realize? You shouldn't.

Many people simply aren't interested in self-realization. I hope that they all find partners who are similarly uninterested so that they can have happy, calm lives together. But as a practitioner, it is your responsibility to create what I call a habitable life. A habitable life is made up of all of the components that support your sad-hana—including proper self-care, right livelihood, and supportive relationships. This is the dharmic recipe for taking care of yourself.

Everyone's spiritual expression is unique, and that expression is going to change over time. If you keep practicing every day, even if you're not practicing much, inevitably your level of desire is going to increase. Self-neglect basically means neglecting that Self that wants to discover a bigger View, that wants more freedom of expression, that wants to find more contentment, whose heart wants to open. That is the self that you should never neglect.

The most pernicious form of self-neglect is when you get a direct message from wisdom, and you ignore it. We all have what Anandamayi Ma called *kheyal*. Kheyal means a spontaneous upsurge of wisdom in the form of an impulse. It's related to improvisational music. You hear a call, and you respond immediately in a skillful, harmonious way. Great improvisational music is a wonder, as is a life lived in musical and graceful response to wisdom.

No matter what our condition, we all have that experience of kheyal. We all have the experience of our own wisdom heart telling us in what direction we should go, what we should do, and what we should not do in any particular moment. Kheyal is an upsurge of inner knowing, of primordial goodness. Following kheyal always leads to spaciousness and relaxation.

All kinds of karmas, tensions, constrictions, and constraints get in the way of us following our kheyal. We hear the instruction of our own wisdom heart, or our teachers, and we start second-guessing ourselves and arguing with ourselves. We ignore the promptings of wisdom because they are inconvenient. We listen to ordinary mind's reasonable-sounding reasons why we can't follow wisdom: "I'm afraid. Someone else won't like it. I'll get criticized. It won't work. I don't have the money, time, etc." But when the wisdom of the heart instructs, whatever it suggests is *always* possible if we just use our courage and creativity.

So the first step in avoiding self-neglect is taking care of your body as best you can, understanding that you are inevitably going to get sick at some point. You don't control everything, but you can make the choice to take care of yourself. Try to align your activities and relationships with what you really want in life. Be brave, and construct a life with your deepest values front and center! Finally, the most subtle and the most difficult thing: follow your wisdom, no matter what. That requires the most clarity and courage of all.

POISON THREE

Over-reliance on individualistic will

One time a friend of mine in academia wrote a book. He was in a difficult marriage and felt unappreciated and disempowered. His comment to me was, "I'm proud that at least I wrote this book on my own."

Of course, if he had thought about it for a moment, he would have realized the falsity of such a claim. In academia, research is based on a field of study to which many people have contributed. We might also ask: who paid him a salary while he was writing the book? Who built the house, the desk, and the computer that supported him in writing the book? Who grew the food that kept him alive? Also, his spouse contributed in myriad ways, not least of which was by taking care of life's administrative tasks and managing their household. The list of those collaborating with this "independent" academic could be endless.

The truth is, we do absolutely nothing independently. We can't take even a single breath without relying on whatever forces give rise to our atmosphere and the continuing respiration of trees. When we seem to make individual decisions, or take independent action, in reality these have been shaped and supported, for better or worse, by our karma, genetics, personality, upbringing, life circumstances, and environment. Our "decision" is only a point in an infinite mandala of cause and effect. We do everything, absolutely everything, in community and in alliance with others.

The laws of the United States and our culture are shaped by the conviction that we are separate, self-willing individuals. Our idea of freedom is that individuals should be able to decide how they will live without "interference" from others. In our everyday lives, we often try not to ask for help. We feel proud when we think we have accomplished something without assistance Even though most of us also value cooperation with others, we value so-called individual independence more.

The Shakyamuni Buddha pointed out that the substrate of our lives is not actually the self-willing individual, but interdependency.[11] Trika Shaivism holds the same View. Rather than being independent, we are more like waves arising from an ocean. A wave is dependent on the ocean. In fact, a wave *is* ocean. A wave has a quasi-individual appearance, but we really cannot tell where it begins or ends.

You may be thinking "that's a no brainer," but consider the pride you feel when you make a claim that you accomplished something on your own without help. Or think about moments when you feel ashamed or humiliated at having to ask for help, or having to admit your dependence on other people. Think about how badly most of us, in the United States, tend to feel if we become incapacitated or impoverished for some reason. We don't like having to ask for help when we fall ill, or when we don't have any money, or because some catastrophe has struck.

All people feel pain when they experience an illness or injury, or suddenly have no money, or lose a home in a hurricane. But here in the United States, we don't just feel pain: we feel humiliated. This is the effect of the poison of our individualistic, prideful culture, a poison that we have mistaken for a virtue.

The shame people feel when things don't work out is the "tell." If you feel ashamed by life's normal ups and downs, your concept of success is at fault. You're like a speeding train that can only move in a straight line. You're going to crash because you are operating as if life does not have curves and switchbacks and mountains. You are convinced you are traveling in one style of landscape, but you are actually moving through a totally different style of landscape. The circumstances of our lives are constantly changing and are largely unpredictable. What is called for is not an unassailable plan or driving ambition, but rather sensitivity, adaptability, and open awareness.

When we live at odds with the fundamental fact that life is uneven, we are going to act without properly taking stock of our situation, asking for appropriate advice, or enlisting the helpers we need. We won't admit when we are lonely, or when things are falling apart, or when we feel overwhelmed. We certainly won't admit that we have taken a wrong turn. This attitude leads to a rougher, more uneven, more isolated life.

Most people recognize that alliances are necessary for success, but people still try to minimize their reliance on others. They strategically manage alliances and feel proud when they get other people to do their bidding. The whole rugged individual narrative includes a kind of cost accounting of human relationships. When you get help from someone, you feel you're in debt to them, and you don't like that. You're trying to be independent! Now you must repay that debt in order to regain your independence.

Certain people in our society have made a lot of money and become famous or powerful at the expense of others and our world. You could say they are successful, but only if you restrict your focus basically to the four inches around their bodies, or maybe to a sphere around their McMansions. If you widen your View, you realize they've been devastatingly unsuccessful. They have caused suffering, destroyed lives, and are in the process of decimating our planet.

Over-reliance on individualistic will causes you to go through life as if you were speeding through the Chunnel, the tunnel under the English Channel that connects the U.K. and France. You're basically speeding along underwater through this tiny, artificially lit tube. You think, "Ha! I got from England to France! I succeeded! Woo hoo!" But your View is exceedingly narrow.

Imagine spending your whole life in a tunnel. That's how it is when our karmas, our compulsions are in the driver's seat. We miss out on all of the relational richness of our world. It's a much lonelier life. It's also a brittle life, a much more fragile life than it might be otherwise because we don't avail ourselves of the wisdom of other people or the wisdom of nature. We're just operating through our karmic drives and trying to get those satisfied. We want to be right about life. We want our decisions to be the right decisions. We can get into this tug of war with life. Life tries to tell us to change our strategy, or adapt, but we keep insisting on our narrow way. That leads to a very uneven, exhausting experience.

Another aspect of living according to individualistic will is that you keep doing stuff you're good at so that you feel good. You over-value proficiency. We are all good at something. So we just repeat that thing and keep feeling good about it and keep getting praise and getting noticed and rewarded. Proficiency is like cocaine. When you are at the top of your game, doing what you feel proficient at, you feel somewhat invincible.

You are like a rat in a cage pressing the bar and getting the cocaine again and again. It's unchallenging. It gives a reward, but the reward is the same every time. Your life doesn't really go anywhere. When you get into those situations, try to notice how much you're just doing the same thing over and over again, simply because you feel comfortably proficient.

I've had this experience many times in my life. It's easy to get that high from being proficient at ordinary stuff. Ultimately, though, it's hollow and boring. I got bored with being good at the same things over and over again. And that kind of disenchantment is a very good thing. It forces you to look elsewhere for fulfillment. I used to cook in restaurants when I was in my twenties. Every night somebody would come and tell me that I was a wonderful cook. At first, I thought it was so fantastic that I cooked these things, and people thought they were wonderful. After about two years, I was like, okay, is this it? I'm going to be here night after night cooking, and people are going to come in and tell me how wonderful my food is, and I'm gonna feel good about it. Is that it? Is that all I want out of life? It doesn't lead anywhere.

We should all be thinking about how we've embodied the rugged individualism narrative. It permeates everything. When we live like this, we are never going to consistently make the choices that are most beneficial to ourselves and others. We just won't take the risks. We won't risk losing face, losing praise, or losing our position, no matter how minor. We won't risk collaborating and being seen by others as we actually are.

Our attempts to defend and reinforce small self give rise to the most fundamental obstacles in spiritual practice. If you approach your practice with the attitude that you're going to succeed at it, that you're going to do it on your own, or that you're going to get what you want, you will never realize. You'll just discover more of the same. Eventually you'll find practice to be extremely frustrating. It will lose all of its glamour because you won't achieve the pre-determined goal, or maybe you will, but that won't bring you the satisfaction you crave. Luckily, this situation often leads to some kind of surrender, and another way of proceeding opens up.

When you finally let nature take your hand and lead *you* instead of attempting to barrel through everything, you discover that, although you are having an individualized *style* of experience, you

43

Poison Three

are not actually an individual. You are continuous with the whole. The experience of being an individual is real, but like the experience of playing a character in a drama is real.

Imagine you are an actor playing a role. When you play a role, that character is being produced within the context of your larger awareness and creative energy. The character is totally dependent on and continuous with you even though it appears to be independent to the viewer. This is each of our situations exactly. God is the player, and we are the played. We are each continuous with the all-encompassing consciousness and energy. If we are doing spiritual practice with too much individualistic will, we are basically saying that we have forgotten our continuity with God. We are insisting on running around in small circles on a small stage. It becomes a frustrating situation if we don't relax and allow the larger wisdom to direct our lives.

If you hang onto your individualistic will too tightly, then often you must fail significantly in order to get unstuck. That's what us spiritual folk call fierce grace. Fierce grace is when reality causes you to lose a job, a person, a home, a community, a teacher, or even your health. Reality destroys your ground so that you are forced to reach out to others, open your heart, and grow. Sometimes it just takes one jolt. I've also known people who keep coming back for more because they aren't ready to stop insisting on having it their way. I hope that won't happen to any of you.

POISON FOUR

Mistaking thinking about life for direct experience

Do you ever notice that when people travel to another country, they tend to return home with a neatly packaged analysis of the cultures they've encountered? Usually the analysis amounts to nothing more than a bundle of clichés. What was "observed" turns out to be not much different from what the person thought before they went. The same old analysis has just acquired an added air of authenticity. Then it is launched on Facebook. You have to wonder if some people who travel have actually gone anywhere!

Many of us are trained to experience life conceptually. We spend our days thinking, planning, analyzing, describing, explaining, critiquing, categorizing, comparing, and narrating. We stockpile clever phrases and "fresh" insights. We deliver our favorite rants.

How many times have you caught yourself saying the same thing in the same way, or rehearsing the same stale responses of glee, outrage, sadness, and so on? We drag these habitual responses out to defend small self and maintain our self-image. If when you encounter a new place, new person, new community, new practice, new situation, or new circumstance, you narrate it in a rote way and respond with habitual emotional reactions, then you're not really being present. You are basically divorced from the livingness of your situation. Your energy is trapped in a small, repeating pattern. There is a lot of energy under tension. Eventually, you start to lose the pathway to a more direct, less mediated palette of discovery, sensation, and energy.

A kind of innocence underlies the circumstance of over-reliance on thinking and conceptualizing. We're so trained to relate to life through mental constructs that our actual lived experience is largely of that. Some of us even have a hard time recognizing that we've lost the capacity to sense fully and to become immersed in livingness. I've noticed that when I talk about immersion or immediacy, many students have a hard time even sensing what that means. Or if they can relate a little bit, they cannot imagine how to bring down the wall of conceptualizing that stands between them and life.

In the direct realization traditions, mind is considered to be a sense organ. The mind is the organ of curiosity. Mind reaches out and into. In fact, the curiosity inherent in all of our senses is an expression of mind. Mind propels each of our senses into directly meeting, exploring, and ultimately integrating with the sensed.

Conceptualizing and intellectualizing are also aspects of curiosity, but stepped down, or contracted. Instead of reaching out to converse, explore, and integrate, we grab at and sequester life, embalming time and circumstance in repeating thoughts and concepts. We can be trained to perform these functions more or less well. We can think more clearly or less clearly, more quickly or less quickly. These qualities of our ordinary intellect give us the appearance of being smart or not. But much of what we call thinking, even very smart thinking, is mostly packaging. Ordinary intellect is more of a packager of reality. This contracted version of curiosity expresses our fear of immediacy and groundlessness, and ultimately expresses our fear of giving up our defense of small self's boundaries.

Theorizing about life is even more stale. We are all trained to perform "what I think-ism," or "what I think-itus." We regularly promote ideas about phenomena about which we know little. We engage our intellect in fancy guesswork or flat out projection and then deploy the results with proud certainty, hoping someone will admire us. Theorizing is a dead thing compared to using your mind to go into reality and touch what's there and discover and be communicated with and learn.

Ordinary mind craves paradigms and scripts. *Satsang* is an ancient and informal kind of spiritual practice. Students sit with their teacher. They ask questions and sing kirtan. During satsang, students often ask me: "What should I do if…?" or "What should I do when…?" or "How should I be when…?" These questions relate to entire classes of unique circumstances. "What should I do if someone calls me and wants to go out with me, and I don't want to go out with them?" Give me a script. Give me a rule to follow.

If we go about our lives as if there are rules to cover every situation, guide our behavior, tell us what to say, tell us how to feel, and tell us what everything means, then we are living through concepts about life rather than relating to life. Then, when life doesn't play according to our rules and scripts, we get upset. We feel disappointed. We feel angry. We feel frustrated. We feel cheated. We feel victimized. We feel left out. We feel many things, but our reactivity has to do with the fact that we had some unconscious or conscious paradigm at work, and life simply ignored us. We have to learn that life is not playing by our rules; it's playing by all the rules all at once.

The psychological View of the human being reinforces these potent scripts about how to feel and respond in different situations. We learn to embody narratives about how to respond to death, trauma, falling in love, growing old, and most other circumstances of human life. We mistake these historically and culturally circumscribed narratives for how we inescapably are, effectively locking the doors of our own cages.

47

Poison Four

You sit down on your meditation cushion, and you are thinking about what you want to happen. You rifle through your grab bag of paradigms about how spiritual practice should progress, and what the outcomes should be. You have some desires going on. You have some egoic compulsions. You sit down with all that baggage, and you're looking around for validation. You're going to feel your kundalini! You're going to be one with everything! Your imagination is working overtime around some little squiggle, or some little flash, or some little flicker. You whip it all up into a fantasy. "Neem Karoli Baba! I think I just saw him!" You have this idea that spiritual awakening is about having visions, or shaking all over, or something like that. You want to be important. You want to be chosen.

You sit day after day, month after month, but you haven't contacted what is actually happening. And then of course spiritual practice becomes very boring and frustrating. Because even though one *can* have kundalini experiences, and even though one *can* have visions, and even though one *can* feel one's continuity with everything, because you are only relating to your concept of those things, you never relax enough to have any direct experience. Relating to fantasy is not the fastest path to waking up, and it is not what our traditions teach us to do. Living through concepts and book learning about spiritual life is not going to bring you the fulfillment for which you yearn.

Every circumstance in life is unique, and the only way to respond skillfully is to be there, with all of your senses open and alive. Spiritual practice gives us the tools to open our senses and drop our conceptualizations, to move through life without any paradigm. In place of the paradigm is wisdom itself. We are guided by the direct apprehension of basic goodness, or wisdom, from moment to moment.

Basic goodness is a term coined by Chögyam Trungpa Rinpoche, the Vajrayana teacher who lived in the 20th century. He defined basic goodness as natural virtue free from conceptual reference points.[12]

Basic goodness and wisdom virtue are different ways of saying the same thing. The natural virtues are not qualities that we possess; they are qualities we inevitably express when karmic impediments have been removed. You could say that the wisdom virtues, or natural virtues, are what make God, God. These are capacities such as compassion, intelligence, creativity, clarity, mercy, generosity, delight, astonishment, joy, and curiosity.

We all have access to basic goodness to some degree. You can recognize it in yourself when you hear and listen to that unerring inner voice that guides you toward what feels wholesome and nourishing in life. Learning how to access basic goodness and how to follow it is the greatest adventure. Following wisdom is where all the juice is. Following your intellectual mind provides stimulation, but no juice. Think of cocaine as compared to ghee.

Many of us are having the experience that our mind is like a wall, or a loud sound, or a mass of humidity, stuck in between us and everything else. You have to cast your life into the river; you have to cast your life into wisdom. You have to utterly abandon preconceptions and focus entirely on the unerring voice of basic goodness, of wisdom. Try to relax conceptual mind, and let in some unpredictable life. Let your experience be whatever it is. Let life teach you whatever it wants to teach you, so that you can actually discover God, rather than trying to dictate to God.

Poison Four

POISON FIVE

Feeling there is a fundamental difference between success and failure

Measuring your self-worth by the yardstick of success or failure is a recipe for great suffering. You succeed and feel elated. Five minutes later, you fail and are full of self-loathing. You are on very shaky ground. Both success and failure are temporary. So your feeling of well-being when you succeed will be temporary also. Success has not relieved your root sense of separation; it has only temporarily appeased your feeling of lack.

No matter how many times you chase success, you will still end up with a feeling of lack at some point or another. You may experience a temporary high, or a temporary feeling of happiness, by succeeding in an ordinary sense. Then it's over, and you are left with the same anxiety about succeeding the next time.

Somebody posted a cartoon on Facebook of an enormous mound of tiny thumbs-up and a person snorting them through a straw. For how many years now have you been checking the numbers of "likes" you get on Facebook? Do you feel any better for having received these thousands of tiny reassurances? A zillion likes are not going to make success stick around. Your fundamental feeling of anxiety about life and your place in it is not going to be assuaged.

When we are anxiously chasing after success and avoiding failure, we expend our vital energy acting in ways that only reinforce our insecurity. We brag about and exaggerate our successes. We even lie about ourselves, or hide aspects of ourselves, in order to make ourselves appear more successful or look better. We try to make others feel less successful in comparison to ourselves. We exacerbate self-doubt and shame when we pump ourselves up in these contrived and dishonest ways.

The only thing we are proving is that we have forgotten that everything is made of wisdom. We have forgotten that we are all God playing whatever part we're playing. We have forgotten that we are an aspect of that continuous consciousness and energy.

The dictum "must succeed, must not fail" is predicated on the existence of an individual, separate from the infinity of cause and effect. It assumes that you alone are responsible for whether some particular action succeeds or fails to result in the desired outcome. This is unreal. You are only a factor in an infinite number of factors. You can try to do your best, but you are not in control of outcomes.

Success and failure are usually defined for you and by you based on ordinary cultural and family karmas. Particular outcomes—usually related to growth or stability—are pre-defined as successful. For instance, staying with your spouse or significant other is generally considered a success, while breaking up is considered a failure. Even if you have many enriching years together, if you ever break up, that is cause for feeling you've failed and for experiencing suffering. But you have not failed if you enjoyed many years of a rich relationship, and you successfully adapted and moved on when the time was ripe.

In the relative sense, we should follow the advice of Krishna in the *Bhagavad Gita*. Just do your best, and let go of the result. In an absolute sense, there are no failures. There are no mistakes, and there are no successes. We know that every painting is made of paint.

This is why we don't feel traumatized when we view a painting of war. Every painting has equality on that fundamental level of being the expression of an artist. Likewise, God's "paint" is consciousness and energy, and we are God's creative expressions.

When we watch an actor in a slapstick comedy trip over something, we don't exclaim, "Oh my God! I hope he's not hurt!" We understand that an actor is playing a part. When we watch movies, we are more lighthearted about people making mistakes and failing. We even find it humorous. We laugh. Watching a drama, we enjoy "tasting" sad feelings. In our everyday lives, God is the actor playing all of the roles. We have just forgotten that.

In our dualistic condition, we cringe with humiliation if we make a mistake, especially a public mistake. We feel terrible about ourselves. Even if we don't feel humiliated, we worry about ourselves. We replay our failings and successes over and over again in our minds. From a relative perspective, the best attitude to develop with respect to success and failure is to try to experience the wisdom that's being expressed in every circumstance. Contemplate what is being communicated and what is being asked of you. Wisdom is always speaking to you.

For instance, circumstances often ask that you exercise modesty, practicality, adaptability, persistence, and patience. Getting what you want in the ordinary sense isn't always the way to develop those virtues. More often, *not* getting what you want is the way. Wisdom often speaks to us through delay and obstruction. Try to act skillfully: understand that you're being worked with and have confidence in this wise reality. If you have this attitude toward failure, then when you *are* experiencing success, you can enjoy a wry little smile. Because now you realize that "little I" getting what it wants is pleasurable, but not absolutely great.

When I can't sense wisdom on my own, I do divination with the *Zhouyi*,[13] an older version of the *Yi Jing* (*I Ching*). The person who taught me how to do divination, Liu Ming, felt that that the ancient Chinese inventors of the oracle probably just kept throwing until they got the answer they wanted. I don't know why he thought that. But you'll find that sometimes, if you keep insisting on getting what you want, you will get what you want. Then that circumstance will draw you into a deeper karmic entanglement. If you insist on getting your own way, wisdom will play with your attachments to success and failure. Failures may reveal wisdom; inappropriately pursued successes may reveal stupidity before they reveal wisdom. It will all become a learning opportunity about cause and effect and letting go, about getting more real, humble, devotional, and determined.

If we can understand that nature is communicating with us, then we can still have our reactivity to successes and failures, but maybe we won't take it all quite so seriously. You don't have to get rid of your reactivity in order to remember View and integrate with presence. That's a very beautiful thing. You don't have to be enlightened in order to get back in touch with enlightened essence nature. You do have to cultivate some distance from your reactivity. You have to be able to recognize what reactivity actually is: a habitual pattern of body, energy, and mind. If you can just leave it alone, then you can continue practicing even though reactivity is arising. You are not suppressing anything. Those habitual forms of emotions and thoughts can do a scary or attractive dance, but you will be doing sadhana. Eventually, everything resolves.

A good word to have in your back pocket is *denaturalization.* Denaturalization means that ordinary habit patterns begin to seem strange. What was once assumed to be natural, right, and inevitable now feels somewhat awkward, like clothing that belongs to someone else. You can see your patterns are something you learned, not who you inevitably are. Then you can be a little bit more detached while you continue practicing.

Right now, many of you feel, "If someone came up on the street and attacked me and robbed me, I would have the right to be angry, and I might even have the right to be traumatized." But being traumatized and getting angry about what other people do is actually a karmic habit pattern, something you've learned.

Poison Five

So you might say, "Screw you! Somebody comes up to me on the street and robs me, I'm gonna be angry, and I'm gonna be victimized, and I'm gonna feel violated, and I'm gonna go to therapy. *It's natural.*" But if you think that one particular response is natural and inevitable, you aren't going to be free. Your responses are conditioned.

For many of us, success and failure are the main organizing principles of our lives. The anxiety that results has also become naturalized. If you are caught up in the drama of appeasing your anxiety about success and failure, you will be distracted. Your clarity will be impaired, and you won't be able to get in touch with a larger wisdom.

Denaturalization pries us away from our habitual reactions to success and failure. But becoming more detached does not mean that we stop feeling emotions such as happiness and sadness. If you are a healer and someone you are treating gets better, feeling happy on their behalf is wonderful. If someone doesn't get better, feeling compassionate sadness on their behalf is a wonderful expression. It means you can treat them beautifully whether they're healing or not healing. But, feeling happy because "I" succeeded in healing, or feeling upset because "I" failed to heal, has nothing to do with other people. That's not a healing situation; that's a conditioned, narcissistic response.

When you have more of an experience of presence and of the intelligence of this reality, then even when you feel uncertain or doubtful or scared, you can still have a lot of confidence in reality itself, in its wisdom. That is not to say that everything will turn out the way you prefer. In fact, it won't. People all over the world are going through wars and natural disasters and personal disasters. But it does mean that no matter what happens, even when life gets terrible, you can still feel that you're being held and guided by this intelligent reality. You can feel that nothing really ever ends. There's really no such thing as ultimate destruction, or ultimate loss or gain.

Poison Five

POISON SIX
Running after pleasure

Many of us chase after pleasure in all areas of life: physical, emotional, and spiritual. When gratifications are delayed, we freak out. Not only do we constantly chase pleasure, but many of us hold the perilous attitude that everything *should* feel good. If circumstances don't feel good, obviously someone must be at fault, either you or the other fellow or even God. We don't want to be physically, emotionally, or spiritually uncomfortable in any way. We have the attitude that when we get into a situation that's even a little bit uncomfortable, we should try to fix it immediately. That's our general attitude here in the U.S., and it leads to people being extremely fragile, brittle, and reactive.

An even more unique circumstance is our constant pursuit of pleasure in the form of approval. We are maniacally concerned about what other people think of us. We want everyone to like us. We never want anyone to be angry with us. We chase approval and praise like heroin addicts chasing after the next fix while ignoring real nourishment. The near-constant effort to be liked and told we are wonderful and amazing is exhausting and can lay waste to an entire life. Our energy can be almost entirely hijacked.

In many cultures, people don't have this kind of infantile relationship to loss, restriction, pain, and discomfort. They don't care so much about admiration. They generally understand that discomfort and pain are part of life. Wiser people everywhere recognize that if you want to have the best possible life, you have to actually be willing to feel pain and discomfort. In fact, oftentimes you must consciously choose to enter into situations of discomfort, pain, or destabilization in order to grow or to be of benefit to others.

Why do so many of us constantly seek pleasure and comfort? It may seem silly to ask this question. After all, pleasure is pleasurable. But the answer to this "silly" question leads right to the heart of reality and our primordial wisdom nature.

The basic urge to pursue pleasure exists on a continuum with the unlimited enjoyment that characterizes the enlightened, unconditioned state. When we compulsively seek enjoyment, even in numbing out and pain, we are expressing the desire to return to essence.

Without exception, we each have primordial memories of the enlightened state. If we didn't have these, we could never realize. We would not know what we are looking for. We would have no yearning for understanding, no longing to return home. We all have an innate knowledge of our real nature. Our access to that knowledge is just more or less blocked by conditioning. All of our pleasure seeking is an effort to recover access to the fullness of our real nature. Our longing to rediscover essence expresses itself at every level of experience, whether we compulsively seek sweet foods, or the sweetness of existence itself.

The urge for constant contact, for constant communication, for feeling good, for feeling pleasure, is not divorced from our primordial connection to the state of divine enjoyment called *ananda*. Ananda means something like bliss plus clarity. It refers to the deep appreciation that this aware, alive reality has for itself and its creations. Reality, aka God, is continually experiencing ananda as it contemplates its unlimited nature reflected in all of creation, including us.

The experience of ananda is related directly to the experience of aesthetic pleasure. If you have ever created anything, you can recall that moment when you stepped back and enjoyed your creation. The sense of wonder, contentment, and pleasure we feel in seeing an aspect of ourselves appear to be external to us, is an echo of the state of God's divine enjoyment.

While reality is enjoying everything without exception, we are looking for pleasure and enjoyment in limited, gross forms. Our ability to experience enjoyment is contracted and compressed. We enjoy this and not that. We compulsively seek certain outcomes and just as compulsively avoid others. We have strong preferences based on what is pleasurable and what is not, according to us.

Our limited comfort and pleasure seeking is not evil or bad or unnatural. In fact, the Supreme Self has fashioned us out of the infinite using limitation as a tool. A ceramist creates a pot by skillfully removing clay from an undifferentiated lump. A sculptor makes a form appear by carving it out of a block of stone. A painter limits the potential of a blob of paint in order to make a painting. A writer chooses only certain words out of the huge number of possibilities in order to create a text. Limitation is the Swiss Army knife of creation.

Furthermore, our limited pleasure and comfort-seeking naturally become less limited when we start to desire a greater understanding of ourselves and reality and, eventually, Self-realization. This magnetizing journey of the return to a less conditioned state and to the recognition of our real nature is the game or sport of the Divine. So limitation is not a problem; it is an aspect of nature expressing and accomplishing itself.

When we begin to wake up, our View of reality enlarges. We have more understanding of the nature of the Self and of our lives. Our senses are more alive and nuanced. We also become less attached to gross forms of pleasure. We are less fearful and more willing to forego temporary, limited pleasures because we have gotten a taste of a more comprehensive pleasure, a more refined and subtle enjoyment. When you have a real experience of ananda, then the gross things that you used to compulsively seek lose their singular allure.

We do not have to fight our attachments to gross pleasures. We do not have to aggressively repel or willfully surrender them. With consistent, sincere daily sadhana, attachments fall away naturally over time. You start to recognize that gross pleasures, comforts, and approval from others are rather uninteresting and limited forms of this *other* thing that you really want a lot more. You are willing to experience temporary fear and discomfort because you realize that these are effects of the slow opening to divine aesthetic enjoyment and clarity.

Sex is a good example of the natural process of leaving the gross behind and discovering what is more subtle and wise. People have different kinds of sexual appetites. Some people cannot feel much of anything unless sex is very intense. Other people cannot relax unless they feel they are under someone else's control. These are only two among an uncountable number of potential arrangements.

Mindless pounding is still some kind of union and expresses some kind of desire to feel more. You can also see that relinquishing control to another is a form of surrender. These circumstances are on a continuum with the desire to wake up, but they are conditioned and contracted expressions of that.

Now, imagine that my senses are open and clear and able to engage intelligently and directly with the infinite banquet of sensory communications. In this circumstance, being pounded mindlessly, or pounding mindlessly, is not going to be very appealing. Imagine also that I already feel deeply relaxed in every circumstance.

I am not going to need to surrender control in order to feel more relaxed. I am not going to need to repeat specific scenarios in order to feel wonderful about sex. As we are waking up, we are less interested in habitual, rote activities. Our level of compulsion radically diminishes.

Another obvious example of this shift can be found in people's attitudes about falling in love. Many people try to be in love with somebody, or try to find a mate with whom they can hunker down and largely ignore the rest of the world. When you begin to get even a glimpse of the unlimited, unconditioned love that this reality is expressing toward everything, you will lose interest in sequestering your love so that it only applies to a few people. You can still have a life partner, but you will love everyone.

If we continue to practice, we inevitably go through stages of disappointment in which the things that were so enticing and magnetizing are no longer so appealing. And then we get dropped off in this blah place for a little while. We can feel weirdly neutral and affectless. The drama and the intensity ratchet down. We aren't used to living life in the middle instead of in the peaks and troughs.

As you go through these same cycles over and over again, you understand that you don't have to worry. You understand that your job is to just keep doing your practice, and let everything keep unfolding. The key is that you have to practice consistently so that you can have a concrete experience of your essence nature, and what it is that you're actually heading toward. You cannot realize armed only with a concept of continuity; you have to experience continuity directly. You cannot progress with a mere concept of divine delight; you must encounter it. No mere idea is going to motivate you to turn away from the immediate pleasures in which you are so immersed and to turn toward the infinity of the creation.

POISON SEVEN

Avoiding pain and fear

The ground shifts a lot when we're practicing. All of the conventions we cling to get challenged, including our conventional and limited ways of relating to others. There are moments that are just terrifying. We also see and experience aspects of ourselves that were previously hidden. The process can be painful. But if you want freedom, you have to be willing to be afraid and in pain at times. You also have to go your own way and not live to the expectations of others. That can also be scary.

The pain I am talking about is not suffering. Suffering is created when there is attachment. The fear and pain we experience while waking up is due to the release of attachment or becoming more aware of attachment. People who go deeply into direct realization traditions such as Trika Shaivism and Dzogchen are generally those who find it a little bit fun to feel destabilized and scared. But then, you know, it always goes further than you bargained for.

I was surprised when I started teaching pranayama. I discovered that some students are anxious, or even terrified, when elongating or holding their breath for only six to ten seconds. There is nothing wrong with their lungs. It is just their fear of death revealing itself. One time, a student was practicing meditation. After a while, he reported to me that he was starting to feel afraid. He was angry at me and at the practice. He felt he had been misled. At first, meditation had helped him to relax, but now he was feeling fear. This was not right, according to him. He also felt like a failure. He had practiced postural yoga diligently for years. He felt quite proud of his accomplishments. But he had never encountered his own fear.

I tried to point out that the fear had always been there and that the meditation was bringing it to the surface. The fact that he was able to feel it represented progress. He didn't accept this. His ego could not digest it. His concept of "meditation" did not include the possibility of feeling fear. He stopped meditating and was angry at me for a while. Eventually, he entered a time in his life when things were falling apart. He was more willing to look at himself. He started meditating and seeking teachings again.

Many people say, "I'm scared, or sad, or angry, so I'm going to stop practicing." Or they say, "I don't feel well, so I'm not going to practice." Or "I'm depressed, so I'm not going to practice." Or, "I'm too distracted, so I'm not going to practice." These are the perfect times to practice! These are the times when effort brings a large result. If you can do practice in the face of the things that normally are your excuses for not doing practice, that is a powerful statement to make and a powerful energetic catalyst. Think of practicing when you are down, distraught, or distracted as a prayer whose determination transmits your deepest desires straight to wisdom.

In our everyday lives, we sometimes take refuge in shame or victimization when things go "wrong." Crisis and disappointment interrupt the smooth climb to the top that we think we deserve, or have defined as the only path to happiness. But feeling badly about yourself is another karmic strategy. It is part of the survival mechanism of small self. "I'm going to fill my time and generate a sense of

Poison Seven

urgency and meaning in my life by feeling really badly about myself. Then I won't have to give anything up, or make any changes because my problem of feeling badly is so all important."

So what do you do when things go south? A lot less than you might imagine. We want to recognize our attachments and how our habit patterns of body, emotions, and mind are arising in response to crisis. But we don't want to get stuck analyzing everything and going deeper into it. That's just a horizontal move on the plane of involvement with our karmic patterns. We are not looking for explanations. We are seeking transformation. In order to transform, we have to redirect energy away from patterns so that the patterns lose momentum.

Instead of going inward and worrying, browbeating, or analyzing anything, turn immediately to your sadhana: to mantra, or meditation, or Guru Yoga, or kriya yoga, or other practices. Or immerse yourself in service to others. Service is a great refuge and a balm. No matter how you are feeling about circumstances or yourself, you can always serve. You can always find concrete ways to assist others in small and large ways. You are redirecting body, energy, and mind when you offer service. Through service, you can get back in touch with primordial goodness, or at least ordinary self-esteem.

We can most fruitfully relate to difficult moments or difficult times by first taking the time to recognize what is happening. When a pattern comes into View, that's when you have an opportunity to redirect your attention and energy. You have no opportunity when you are being unconsciously driven by karmic conditioning. But when circumstances cause patterns to resurface, that is the best time to bring awareness and energy to your practice.

Don't shove self-revelations of karmas out of the way, or try to wage war against them, or numb yourself out with various distractions. Limiting karmas are just like annoying houseguests. What do you do when you have annoying houseguests? Well, what I do is try to pay as little attention to them as possible while still being friendly and polite. If you have a houseguest who is not jibing with whatever the scene is at your house, you still want to be hospitable and kind. You don't want to be aggressive. But you're not going to say, "Let's go out and spend the whole day together!" You're going be like, "I have a little bit of work to do this morning. I'll be done around noon, and then maybe we can catch a quick lunch, and it will be fun to invite some more people over this afternoon."

Our attachments are temporary visitors; they're not our essence nature. So we shouldn't grab onto them and treat them as if we're going to spend the rest of our lives together. We should just go about putting our energy into our real business in life—waking up—while our scary karmas do their scary dance. That's actually the best strategy.

The Daoists have an expression: Don't fight the tigers. Think of your myriad strategies for avoiding pain and fear as tigers on a jungle path. If you are walking in a forest and a tiger jumps out at you from the side of the road, don't stop to fight the tiger. Go around the tiger if possible. But also don't shout out, "I'm going around you!" Tiptoe around, and you will have a better chance of surviving.

Our real condition, however much we don't like it, is the *only* possible starting point for having an authentic spiritual life. If you discover that you have fear, you have discovered what you have to work with. You can get really sad about yourself because you see something, or you get really angry at the teacher because something happened that you weren't expecting. All those things are actually early fruits of the practice.

We encounter obstacles, but this does not mean that we're condemning ourselves to a lifetime of practicing and feeling horrible. Spiritual life is not all fear and pain. And it's not working only when it's uncomfortable. I mean nobody would do this if that were the case. Don't get some idea that the badge of a true yogi is that you're just uncomfortable all of the time.

However, you won't really get to anything other than mild, ordinary relaxation if you're not willing to go through some of the more painful, fearful things. Usually, when people start meditating, or doing pranayama or mantra, it is fun and relaxing. If they keep at it, they get rewarded with different kinds of experiences, including a moderate quantity of boredom, physical and emotional discomfort, and fear. Occasionally people simply refuse to feel uncomfortable, they refuse to tolerate it, they refuse to let it happen, and so they stop practicing. This is my father's condition. My father is an anxious person. He tried meditation one time and experienced his own anxiety without the buffer of his usual distractions. That was it for him. He never tried it again.

When you get to that place of fear or pain, you *could* experience the crumbling of false self-image. So if you stop doing the practice, you basically are saying "I refuse to work with my real condition because my real condition isn't the condition I want!" The truth is: if your practice isn't disturbing to you at times, you aren't really going very deep. The sign of a stalled practice is that it always feels good, or it's never scary, or it's never disappointing or boring. Then you're a drifter. You're like a leaf floating on water. Or you're like someone floating in a lake. The water is really nice and warm on the top, so you decide "I'll just stay up here. I'm not putting my foot down in the cold, deep darkness." It's always a little scary putting your feet down in a deep lake, isn't it? Practice is the same way. Reality is deep and wide.

We need courage and a little confidence. The confidence comes from what your own inner wisdom recognizes in the teacher and the teachings and from doing the practice. If you keep doing sadhana, eventually you are going to learn more about how the process of waking up works. Then it will be easier to look in the mirror. You will understand the necessity of seeing clearly and will also understand that you are fine, karmas and all. You won't feel so angry or distraught about your limitations. You won't feel as if something unfair has happened to you. You may even begin to develop a "bring it on" attitude because you will understand that you can't release what you refuse to acknowledge.

POISON EIGHT

Mistaking good and bad and right and wrong for absolutes

The terms absolute and relative teachings, or Views of reality, are borrowed from Buddhism. We also could say absolute and relative experience. In Trika Shaivism, on the other hand, we use the words dualistic, or limited, and supreme. Relative, dualistic, and limited all refer to our ordinary experience: how things seem and feel to us from moment to moment when we are not particularly realized. Absolute and supreme refer to the enlightened experience, unconditioned by time, form, and circumstance.

In some traditions, particularly in Buddhist traditions, students receive the relative teachings first. Much later, if ever, they receive the absolute teachings. A typical relative teaching is that we should watch our minds. This teaching is relative to our dualistic, limited condition. An absolute teaching is that we should unmind the mind. According to some traditions, absolute teachings pertain only to students in a less limited condition. In Trika and other direct realization traditions such as Dzogchen, absolute or supreme teachings are generally given first, and immediately after, the relative teachings.

The direct realization method advances from the understanding that the absolute teachings serve as the larger context for the relative. In the same way, our real, unconditioned nature is the larger context for our limitations and fixations. Big View serves as a beacon as we move through our everyday lives, working on the relative most of the time. We do all of our ordinary work with the absolute as a reminder of where we are going. We also don't want to get stuck by mistaking the relative for the absolute. So we want to know about the nature of the ultimate reality from the beginning.

More importantly, perhaps, we recognize that each student is in a unique condition. It may be that some students are able to understand and benefit from more expansive, subtle teachings and practices right from the beginning. The general method in Trika Shaivism is to offer more subtle methods along with more accessible methods. Students can then experiment and discover what works best for them.

Knowing about the ultimate reality does not mean intellectual or philosophical understanding. Even in our limited condition, we can have a real experience of essence nature. Being around the teacher, receiving transmission, and doing different kinds of sadhana give you the opportunity to have direct experience. Then the beacon becomes very real. It's something you're actually sensing, something concrete. It's not just a distant fantasy or intellectual notion.

Our concepts of good and bad and right and wrong are firmly in the zone of dualistic, relative View and teachings. They do not accurately or fully reflect the supreme reality. As spiritual practitioners, when we have this more limited View, we do need precepts and rules and guidelines. These help us to approximate being skillful when we are not able to be naturally skillful all the time. However, we should not get fanatical about our rules. We should follow them with the larger View in mind.

Let's start with an easy example. Maybe you think liver is terrible. You hate liver and think it tastes disgusting. If you believe that liver inherently sucks, you are an everyday fanatic. But hopefully, you understand that someone else loves liver. And you understand that some other person won't eat it because it comes from an animal, and yet another person won't eat it because it is not very aesthetically enticing. Finally, a different person might enjoy fond childhood memories of eating liver. They eat liver because they enjoy the feeling of nostalgia associated with it. So you understand that your loathing of liver is relative to your condition. If you understand absolute View, you know that nothing inherently sucks, not even liver.

We are a little more fanatical about, say, murder. You might strongly believe that murder is wrong. We derive comfort from these kinds of dogmatic ways of navigating the world. But murder is not always wrong. Someone I know witnessed this scene in India in a train station. A person was wandering around on the tracks and got hit by a train. He was at death's door, in terrible pain, his skull cracked open. Understanding that no help would arrive, some old guy with a stick came along, hopped down into the track, and finished the job by bashing the guy in the head with the stick. This was compassion, not murderous evil.

Every situation is like this. There are only circumstances in which we can act more or less skillfully. We can start by acknowledging that there are always circumstances in which something we think is terrible is actually fine, and something we think is fine is actually terrible. From a relative perspective, each situation is unique and arises through a unique and infinite web of cause and effect. We cannot apply rigid paradigms of right and wrong and good and bad and expect to be skillful in our responses.

I've always hoped that I would be able to act as compassionately as the old man with the stick if the time came. Then one day some years ago, also in India, a dog got hit by a taxi near where I was staying. Its rear legs were broken, and it couldn't walk to find food. I'm sure it had other injuries. Stray dogs are the lowest of the low in India. So of course, no one helped the poor dog. But I couldn't bring myself to kill it. That was selfishness.

Until we are more awake, our View is extremely limited. Our ideas of good and bad, right and wrong derive from our relativistic experience, our conventional mind, and our karmas, including patterns of belief inherited from our families and cultures. But we tend to forget that our vision is limited. In fact, we are trained to feel superficially more certain about things than we actually are upon deeper investigation.

From a relative perspective, spiritual practice helps us to become more openhearted. In the direct realization traditions specifically, we practice to discover greater freedom of self-expression. We are trying to share our best with others. We want to end our own suffering and the suffering of others. From the supreme View, there is only auspiciousness. Auspiciousness refers to the direct experience that, despite our suffering, all that exists is made of wisdom virtue. This is identical to saying everything is God, or everything is essence nature, or everything is Shiva Nature, or everything is consciousness, or everything is Buddha nature, or everything is Christ consciousness, or any number of other similar formulations. God is all, and God is wisdom virtue. Wisdom virtue means beneficence, mercy, compassion, devotion, self-love, intelligence, creativity, curiosity, clarity, and equanimity. These wisdom virtues are not attributes of the supreme reality: they *are* the supreme reality.

People sometimes like to claim that they love another person unconditionally, perhaps a partner, or a child, or a friend. But their love *is* conditioned. It is conditioned on it being that specific person. Our love and our compassion are limited by ideas of right and wrong, good and bad. From a dualistic perspective, loving all beings, no matter how they are showing up, might be deemed crazy.

Poison Eight

Should I love a criminal? Should I love a dictator? Should I love a poisonous spider? Should I feel compassion for a person who wrongs me or hurts me? From our relative View, we decide who is deserving and who is not. But God's compassion is absolute. It has no boundaries, no reason or explanation, and no justification. It flows out endlessly, like a mighty river from the open sky of awareness, blessing everyone equally.

Our lives are organized around binaries of right and wrong, good and bad. These oppositions help to manufacture our sense of importance. They are used to defend our self-image, our sense of individuality, and various boundaries including national and religious boundaries. As oppositional pairs, they support fanaticism of both the everyday and grand varieties. But these binaries are *always* dependent on each other and on circumstance. The goodness of existence, of God, of our real nature, has no opposite, and it is not dependent on anything. Primordial goodness is not a position or an idea: it is the palpable presence that infuses all of reality. This is what we discover in ourselves, and everywhere, as we begin to wake up.

Poison Eight

POISON NINE

Mistaking temporary appeasements for the goal

Anandamayi Ma said, "You must be careful not to be satisfied at any stage and so get stuck."[14] Dissatisfaction is a non-enlightened person's best friend. This is why Saturn's influence is so good for practitioners. Saturn brings that heavy, uncomfortable intuition that something is not right. We need at least some dissatisfaction. If we're not dissatisfied, we are not going to try to change our situation.

We all feel temporarily satisfied with temporary appeasements. In fact, we put a lot of emotional, physical, and mental resources into chasing temporary pleasures and comforts. After some, usually short, period of time feeling satisfied, we start chasing that same satisfaction again, and then again. You could say that our entire relationship to satisfaction is like eating a bag of potato chips. Until the bag is empty, or until we become dissatisfied with munching one potato chip after another, we will keep going back.

In the Tantrik traditions, we say "you rise by that which you fall." Anandamayi Ma taught that "the ground whereon one falls and gets hurt, with the help of that same ground one tries to get up."[15] We try to repurpose our relentless drive to seek fulfillment. We recognize that this drive will eventually lead us to want to do spiritual practice. Slowly we replace chasing temporary appeasements with chasing the eternal.

I advise students to make their practice spaces as beautiful as possible in order to stimulate the desire to sit down. Our tradition affords us many sensory enticements to practice. We enjoy colorful fabric, incense, bells, pictures, statues, flowers, music, and beautiful cups and offering trays. These accessories magnetize our body, energy, and mind. Later on, that's not so important because we start to perceive the jewel-like quality of reality itself. The external enticements are only living symbols of *that*.

When we experience ordinary mind's satisfaction with temporary accomplishments and acquisitions, we are momentarily convinced that those are what we were looking for all along. "I finally got the house, the partner, the job, the perfect food, the drug... this is it!"

When I first went to graduate school, I thought, "Wow! Academia is great! I get paid to read and write." I was happy. I remember telling a friend, "They're going to have to drag me out of here feet-first. I'm never leaving this place." Then a few years later, I was over it, and I walked out. No dragging required. Yet for some period of time, I was totally convinced that a life in academia was the answer. Luckily my practice showed me otherwise. Not that as you wake up a little you couldn't stay in an academic job and be fine with it, but you would no longer think "Oh...this is the be-all, end-all! I've arrived!"

We practitioners mistake temporary appeasements for the goal when we are attached to a limited, and in some sense fantasy, understanding of what waking up looks and feels like. We set spiritual goals based on our limited understanding. This happens more often than not. For instance, your idea of the goal of meditation may be that it should help you to become more efficient at work, or it should calm you down. Then you only do a little bit of practice to achieve this result, and you delay or never get to the deeper transformations and discoveries.

You might be in a spiritual lineage with a strong concept of enlightenment. One of the ideas about enlightenment is that your mind becomes free of thoughts. You'll hear this kind of thing in both Buddhist and Hindu teachings. Then there is the infamous kundalini. When it rises, you are enlightened. *Voila.* Presumably. Another idea is that you take a light body. When an accomplished person dies, their body may become very subtle and give off a display of the lights of the five elements. This concept of enlightenment is more common in Tibetan traditions.

Try to remind yourself that any goal you have predefined before you do the practice is going to end up being a mistaken or at least a limited goal. If you insist on your goal, you might get stuck with achieving that goal. Even if you convince yourself that you are enlightened, eventually you will recognize the limitations of your condition. Nothing you can dream up, and certainly nothing you can get attached to, is going to be near what reality offers you if you practice with no goal other than to find out.

Everything of lasting value in my practice has come as a total surprise. We can read books and get teachings, but we can only know what happens by walking the path day by day. Self-realization is not an experience. It's not a state. I'm convinced that after a certain point, anyone with a high degree of realization would have zero interest in defining it. They certainly would not view it as an individual, heroic accomplishment.

We should practice without any goal other than to wake up and discover what's here. Try not to settle on anything. Try not to be settled on your idea of the path. Try to hold the attitude that you are going to be surprised.

As practitioners, we want to be able to enjoy everything. We want to be able to find satisfaction in everything. We want to be content with everything, and that takes tremendous transformation of our senses and our perceptions and our understandings. To find contentment, or beauty, or enjoyment in everything—even in sorrow, even in all the different appearings in our world—that's no small thing.

If our longing is weak, it won't carry us that distance. We'll just pause somewhere and hang out. We'll accept some lesser appeasement, some lesser satisfaction for a while, maybe a long while. Only desire can make us insist on not getting stuck.

Trying to manufacture permanence within the experience of impermanence sends us on detours. Even if you are mired in attachments to impermanent things, try to have clarity about what is driving you. Don't follow your compulsions unconsciously. What is it that you find yourself continually repeating? Being able to see clearly that you are trying to hold onto something fleeting, and that it won't ultimately satisfy you, is a great first step. Whatever you are holding onto has actually got *you* in its grip.

Unfortunately, if you have strong, driving desires shaping your experience such as, "I want this; I want that; I need this; I need that," you can't just order them to go away. Karma rarely resolves quickly. So keep the bigger View in mind even though you still feel the desire for those temporary appeasements. Keep the View that whatever you are chasing doesn't offer you permanent release from your loneliness, your sense of anxiety about your life, your feeling that you aren't safe, your feeling that you aren't good enough. Keep in your mind, even as you are following various karmic compulsions, that in order to obtain that temporary appeasement, you're going to have to repeat the chase over and over and over again. Keep in mind that if you keep practicing, eventually you will begin to have a more sustained experience of eternal presence: the intelligence and energy of existence itself. Then you will stop suffering. You will regain your capacity to enjoy the beauty and diversity and even the fleetingness of impermanence.

This method is like reminding yourself about the possibility of health as you're going to a fast-food restaurant because you're feeling this compulsion to eat bad food. The food will fill you, and all that salt and fat and sugar will provide some temporary satisfaction, but it isn't actually going to nourish you in the proper way. Even so, by reminding yourself of health, you are making the effort not to eat totally unconsciously.

Even though dissatisfaction is bad news on one level, it is great news on another. If we could find permanent satisfaction in ordinary appeasements, there would be no spiritual growth. Luckily for us, every temporary feeling of contentment eventually dissipates and leads to the re-arousal of dissatisfaction. The process is inevitable and natural. The only question is: when and how will that inevitable dissatisfaction lead us to start moving with greater determination and awareness toward the eternal?

MEDICINES

MEDICINE ONE
Being forced to recognize the intrinsic value of others

Medicine, as I'm using it here, indicates a circumstance that brings grace into our lives. Grace means that circumstances conspire to open us to greater wisdom. We are able to recognize something we couldn't recognize before. A freshness enters into our sense perceptions. Our View expands. Our hearts open. The medicines often function through bottoming out. A fixation that was supporting us and allowing us to function in some pseudo-normal way just stops working. Then we have to look outside of our fixation to get help, or to find a solution. The medicines are sometimes bitter. They're often confrontational. They are processes that force us to look at what we previously avoided seeing.

In a wonderful passage in the *Vijñana Bhairava Tantra*, Bhairava (Lord Shiva) is talking to Bhairavi (Shakti).[16] For the benefit of the student reading the text, Bhairavi is playing the role of the student of Bhairava. In answer to her questions and "doubts," Bhairava implies that Bhairavi's View is too narrow. Bhairavi must let go of some attachments to her habitual ways of relating to and understanding spiritual life. In our everyday lives, many of us want to avoid looking unflinchingly at our real situation for as long as we possibly can. We want to pretty it up, or numb ourselves out. Seeing how things actually are can be painful. At times, circumstances themselves force us to take the rather bitter medicine of clear seeing. But whether sweet or bitter, the medicines are all grace.

When I was in my early twenties, I was quite snobby, particularly intellectually. I didn't grow up rich. In fact, my family was rather lower middle class, or as I later defined us, "bohemian class." My parents didn't have much money, but they were both artists. We had a lot of cultural capital, and I was snobby about that.

My father would sometimes say, "If you aren't an artist, your life is worthless." This is the sort of competitive atmosphere in which I grew up. I learned to categorize people into the "interesting" people and the "boring" people. I didn't pay much attention to the so-called boring people. I didn't engage much with people in the checkout line, or just random people.

Then I became involved romantically with someone who had substance abuse problems. When things got bad, I went to Al-Anon. It's a group for supporting friends and family of people who have alcohol and other substance abuse issues. I found myself sitting in rooms with people from all walks of life, listening to everything that they had to say, and hearing wisdom from all of these different kinds of people. Receiving valuable insights from "boring" people, insights that were helpful and compassionate, really changed my life. I had a deep recognition of the intrinsic value of other people. This was a transformative experience for me. I became less self-concerned than I had been before. I was less wrapped up in myself. I started asking more questions. I became more curious about different kinds of people. I had always been curious, but in a narrower way.

When we look at our patterns of body, emotions, and mind—the things that repeat themselves compulsively—they are like viruses. They are entities that have very few characteristics. As whole people, we are complex and nuanced. We have richness and depth, but our fixations constantly run the same anxiety, the same need, the same demand, over and over again. In order to survive, they have to eat our own and other people's energy.

Anxiety about yourself, attachment to self-image, and just being wrapped up in yourself is *always* at the expense of other people's energy. When we're overly self-concerned, we're trying to get something—love, attention, or reassurance. Maybe we are trying to win, or be right and reassure ourselves of our superiority. We're being defensive or aggressive. We aren't perceiving, listening, or responding properly.

When we are anxious about ourselves, we may look as if we are talking to another person. We may look as if we're being intimate with somebody, but actually we are relating to another person as a bit player in the drama of our own karmas. So, for this reason, any kind of undue self-concern is always at the expense of recognizing and relating to the unique dimension, integrity, and intrinsic value of the other person.

Our self-concern sucks energy out of others. It harms other people when we are hijacking the energy of our relationships to fuel our fixations. It's harmful when I demand that you listen to me talk about the same problem I've been talking about for the last twelve years. It's harmful when I rope you into my chronic anger, my chronic sadness, my chronic disappointment, my competitiveness, my anxiety about money, my seduction. It's harmful when I demand that you participate on my terms.

Let's say I am habitually disappointed in the behavior of other people. I am going to demand that you participate in my disappointment as if other people actually *are* disappointing. I am not going to take responsibility and acknowledge that I am manufacturing disappointment in order to express my feelings about my own life and possibly get a fix of feeling superior. Because I'm attached to my limited karmic vision, I won't acknowledge that I might not be experiencing others with clarity. If you want to recognize the unique dimension of other people, you have to notice that other people actually exist apart from your needs. You have to recognize that other people don't owe you their energy to support your fixations. And then, if you are lucky, you'll get into a situation in which you are forced to recognize the intrinsic value of other people. That can be hugely healing and help to relieve you of some of your own karmic burden.

Of course, we're talking on a relative level right now about the experience of discovering that everyone has intrinsic value and how that discovery can kind of shock us out of our suffocating self-concern. We all must work at the relative level to widen our sphere of curiosity and concern. A spiritual community helps you to do that. You get thrown in with people who are not handpicked by you. Over time, if you keep doing practice and you stick around long enough, you learn, sometimes painfully, to love all of the people in your community regardless of how they are showing up. Through this natural process, you begin to include more people and beings in your life outside of your community.

On the absolute level, when we begin to wake up more, we begin to directly perceive the jewel-like quality of everything. We begin to appreciate the creativity and expressivity of the variety of different kinds of people, even people who we might condemn, who do heinous things, even people who hate other people. When our inner eyes begin to open, we can appreciate all peoples' intrinsic value, recognizing that we are all made of the same adamantine Self.

In other words, on an absolute level, intrinsic value isn't conditional. It's not just because someone says something wise, or because they help us, or because we see something interesting about them. Even if our field of interest widens, and we include more people in it, that is still very much on a relative level. But as our inner eyes are opening, and our subtle senses are opening, and we are really perceiving the intrinsic value of everyone and everything, then we are also inevitably perceiving *our own intrinsic value*. At that point, we lose our attachment to self-image.

Many of us really don't look at other people as having intrinsic value because we're not so sure about our own worth. A lot of this insecurity has to do with the competitive atmosphere that we live in. Everyone, of course, has the same intrinsic value, but we don't recognize that because we're not really so convinced of our own intrinsic value. We certainly aren't focused on the intrinsic value of other people: their wisdom, their beauty, the creative way they're showing up.

When we recognize that our own intrinsic value is perfect and indestructible, we realize that there is nothing to massage or promote or defend. Our essence nature can't be improved upon, and it doesn't need defending. We can only have an experience of improving upon our relative experience. When we recognize that, the anxiety that underlies self-concern begins to radically dissipate.

MEDICINE TWO

Feeling horror at the arising and slipping away of opportunity

Opportunity means an opportunity to let go of something; or an opportunity to learn something directly from wisdom; or an opportunity to move differently so that a situation goes in a better way for your own health and spiritual unfolding, and for other people's as well. When we begin to wake up, our senses, including our minds, open and refine. We actually perceive the promptings of wisdom more consistently. Yet often we don't listen, and then we miss opportunity. As we go along, we become more acutely aware of the consequences of following fixation rather than wisdom. The more aware we are, the more painful and poignant is our experience of missing opportunity.

An alive, self-aware reality conspires to relieve us of karmic conditioning both by placing obstacles in our path and by providing the tools we need to resolve obstacles. This process is just like a game app. The game starts off easy, and the tools are few. When we develop skill, the game gives us harder obstacles, and the tools get more plentiful and sophisticated. Sometimes we notice the tools and use them skillfully. Sometimes we act unskillfully and have to try again. At other times, we're so unconscious, we don't even recognize an obstacle *or* remember our tools.

The game of sadhana helps us to relax our conceptual way of relating to life, relax our dogma, and relax our self-defensiveness. We start off playing a conventional game. We measure our progress, strive to destroy obstacles, and yearn for particular rewards. Eventually we switch to playing in "endless" mode. At this point, the game becomes an objectless, goal-less dance of grace.

Ordinary mind represents a relative state of unconsciousness. We are driving ourselves along with a conventional set of assumptions about what an individual is and about what we should be doing with our lives. Our relationship to obstacles and the loss of opportunity is also conventional. We want to get the job, but the person interviewing us gives us a hard time. Maybe we didn't get a good enough reference, or maybe we got into a traffic accident and are late for our job interview and the interviewer is annoyed with us. We interpret this kind of obstacle and loss of opportunity in a very conventional way.

We complain about our bad luck, or we think that the world is out to get us, or we are being punished, or people are unfair, or something like that. Then we go through the whole range of conventional emotional reactivity. We're upset. We're angry. We get aggressive. We're going to push through those obstacles. We're going to get what we want come hell or high water. Or we are sad and ashamed, and we withdraw.

We often live in this extremely brittle, reactive way. When we start to do practice, we become a little more sensitive. We gain some clarity about how things actually work. We start to have a bigger View. We start to understand, even in just a conventional sense, that all happenstance has infinite causes and effects.

Why did your friend misunderstand you in some moment? Why did you become frustrated when you couldn't get your point across?

You could say that your friend is being a jerk, or stupid, or maybe you weren't at your best and didn't express yourself well. But then you could widen your View and ask why was that person talking to *you* at that particular moment. And what caused that person to be born in the same time-space as you? And why were you not at your best on that day?

Even in a conventional sense, these questions are ultimately unanswerable. The more "whys," the more our view of the field of karma expands. The horizon of the field of cause and effect keeps receding. While we cannot come up with an ultimate explanation as to why a certain thing happens in a certain way at a specific time, we *can* feel time. We *can* feel the energy and wisdom of each moment with our senses and minds. We *can* have a more subtle, palpable, and usable experience of cause and effect. This is all that is required because the energy and wisdom of the moment takes into account all circumstances and all causes and effects.

Using our senses and our minds to reach directly into the living presence of the present, we can know when we are in danger of missing opportunities and how we might act and choose more skill-fully. Most of us can feel the subtle promptings of wisdom to some degree already, but we just aren't paying enough attention. We can also look back and recognize particular moments when we acted unconsciously, and our current situation began to develop. We can recognize when we had an impulse to do the right thing, and we ignored it. Sadhana subtilizes our senses so that we can choose and act according to wisdom before it is in the rear-view mirror. We begin to sense and see the bigger arrangement as it is developing.

Real skillfulness is not about becoming a better strategist in your life. Whether you're a poor strategist, an okay strategist, or a master strategist, that is all on a horizontal plane. It's all very ordinary. The point is, we have the innate capacity to open our senses in a non-ordinary way. We can begin to really sense that our total circumstance is communicating with us, and that there is wisdom in those communications. We can feel for skillful timing in a concrete way. In some cultures, this would be a no-brainer. Here in the u.s., we are not used to thinking this way. Or if we are, we're very New-Agey and conceptual about it.

Every person, of any sensitivity, has the real experience every now and then of being guided to move in one direction or another. Or you get a sense that patience is appropriate in a particular situation. You sense whether to wait or move ahead. When you start to open up your senses and your perceptions by doing practices such as meditation and mantra, you have these kinds of experience much more of the time. You come to understand that you are living in an ocean of communication. Right now, of course, we are living in an electronic ocean of communication. Understand that what is going on at the gross level is a direct expression of the more subtle. As above, so below. This reality loves to communicate.

At the same time, we still have a lot of compulsion: moments of being abducted by the momentum of our karmic patterns, our conditioning. Until we are more realized, our experience of wisdom and compulsion is that of two flows moving in opposite directions at the same time. A lot of us can relate to this when it comes to our health, or our relationships with other people. These are two areas in which we experience a lot of conditioning. When we start to notice that wisdom is communicating with us, we start to understand that we often make choices based on karmic momentum.

As we become more aware, we more strongly and immediately feel the responses we get from our bodies and circumstances when we indulge in habitually repeating patterns. These responses may or may not actually be stronger. Maybe we are just noticing them for the first time, or are feeling them more deeply. Our hearing and clarity of seeing and ability to sense more subtle energetic "touches" all begin to bring us more clues about arising opportunities. We really start to understand how our suffering might have been avoided. We can see the long stretch of how we got here, but we're still not sure if we're going to find our way out. This is both painful and awesome.

87

Medicine Two

We can get into situations of experiencing the horror of watching opportunity arise and slip away. We see opportunity, and yet somehow, in some circumstances, we're just not ready to follow. But the more disturbed we feel about missing opportunities, the harder we are going to try to follow wisdom. That is why our distress is a medicine.

In general we could say that the definition of missing opportunity is going in an adharmic direction. *Adharmic* means not dharmic. Anandamayi Ma said: "What is dharma? Those actions which are conducive for attaining the Supreme Self. That is desirable for everyone. This is also the natural way of life. Sorrows are due to unnatural ways. So that is adharma."[17]

Adharma means whatever is not proper for a human being and for our particular circumstances. Adharma is anything affecting our body, energy and mind that leads to more entanglement, more difficulties, more enervation. Every situation has many doors through which we could walk, or which we could bang into! But in the tradition of Trika Shaivism, we are not thinking one door is good, and the others are bad, or sinful. Our approach is practical and functional. We want to always try to follow wisdom toward whatever is "conducive for attaining the Supreme Self."

As you go along waking up more, you enter a period in which that feeling of lost opportunity, of walking through an adharmic door is very painful. And this eventually motivates you to work harder to pull yourself out of your karmic compulsion and go in the direction of wisdom. This is an important time in your spiritual development. The world conversation is becoming more apparent to you, and you realize how much you've basically been screwing up and how many opportunities you've missed.

I remember very clearly going through this. I was just horrified at the numbers of mistakes that a human being could make in not following wisdom! The infinite web of cause and effect was just starting to become known to me. I felt overwhelmed and nearly paralyzed.

Everything seemed so vast and complicated. I felt like the proverbial bull in an infinite china shop.

I went to visit a friend of mine who is an accomplished Buddhist practitioner. I was quite upset and crying about this "terrible" situation of not wanting to make mistakes. He waited for me to finish up with my self-pity session. Then he said, "You expect me to feel sorry for you about that?"

Eventually, I gained enough spiritual understanding to recognize that the whole concept of mistakes is mistaken. That spurred me to work very, very hard to commit myself more firmly to following directly perceived wisdom whenever and however it arose. Despite the fact that I was born into a Jewish family, I have always lived in a largely Christian culture. I hadn't escaped internalizing the feeling that if I made a mistake, I was going to get into trouble with God. The Trika View is based on the experience of continuity with God, not difference. The same Self is playing all parts, and so from the absolute perspective, there is no other to punish.

MEDICINE THREE

Feeling overwhelmed by circumstances and being forced to ask for help

Becoming overwhelmed by circumstance means that your conventional ways of dealing with things break down. You can't digest what's happening using ordinary mind and ordinary means. You feel that things are falling apart, and you can't cope. Then what happens? You find other resources and capacities that you didn't know you possessed or had long ignored. You realize your interdependency with others. You ask for help.

Reality regularly arranges for us to experience overwhelm. A classic example would be when people encounter a large-scale disaster. People who anxiously guard their time, homes and possessions, or even their friendliness, relax their boundaries in order to help strangers. A feeling of comradery prevails. Some people say that the 9/11 terrorist events in New York changed the character of that city, rendering it a more friendly and supportive place to live.

Every person at some point gets into a life situation, even a terrible life situation, in which something is breaking down and falling apart. You lose your job, or your partner walks out on you, or a beloved person dies, or you get injured, or a natural or man-made disaster overtakes your life. Most people find that, after they fall apart, they can go to a deeper place and discover new inner resources. They discover deeper relationships with the people who care about them, or even experience the kindness of strangers. They find themselves willing, at least temporarily, to try new approaches. And they find out that being in alliance with other people is crucial for survival and happiness.

Many of us generate a feeling of pride by holding the false idea that we've done something on our own without help from other people. This is completely erroneous. We do not breathe a single breath of air without the collaboration and support of an entire planet. The idea that we do anything alone is ludicrous. In order to take pride in this ludicrous idea, we have to be looking at the world through foggy glasses with 360-degree blinders. We have to *not* see all of the people who made the tools we used to achieve our great, solo accomplishments. We have to unsee all of the people involved in housing, feeding, and paying us. We have to not see all of the people who came before us and developed the skills and knowledge we are using in accomplishing our goals and maintaining our lives. I could go on, but you get the point.

Being in a crisis really breaks down that isolationist attitude. We become at least temporarily aware of our fragility and of our need for alliances with others. Hopefully, our new awareness is *not* temporary. But for some people, once the feeling of being over-whelmed subsides, they ramp up the attempt to reconstruct things along pre-crisis lines. Once the situation becomes more manage-able, they will attempt to re-establish their old ways of dealing with life. They will still be their competitive, prideful selves. They will still be anxiously chasing the same things. They will still be trying to maintain a sense of self that is artificially independent.

In direct realization traditions such as Trika Shaivism, one of the teaching methods is to deliberately create circumstances in which

91

Medicine Three

students experience a feeling of being overwhelmed. The point of being intentionally overwhelmed in a spiritual context is so that you *don't* rebuild. It's so that you can acclimatize to proceeding in the raw, without your usual conceptual, karmic apparatus shielding you. When boundaries break down, you experience a more natural openness, and you have more possibility to realize your continuity with life.

In a sense, the teachings and the circumstances surrounding the teacher put you in the position of having to wing it, over and over, and over again. The good news is that enlightened experience is basically one hundred percent winging it. There's no strategy, there's no prophylactic planning. Of course, everyone has to plan something or other. I'm not talking about just how to get something done. But being in a more awake state means residing in total responsivity to immediate circumstances and adapting with total ease, come what may. We are not trying to map out and fix the future.

Most of us have cobbled together some kind of habitable persona. Even if it's barely working, we are still very attached to our self-concept and patterns of body, energy, and mind. We will try to make it all work for as long as possible. Even if we begin a spiritual practice, we will compartmentalize our practice so that it has as little effect as possible on our karmic patterns.

We are like a middle-aged person in a stale marriage. Our spiritual practice is the affair we are having just to release some tension. But we will never willingly leave our marriage, even if things get really bad. We cling to the devil we know. Then some Tantrik teacher comes along and starts messing up our compartments, our excuses, our whole self-concept.

When you are overwhelmed, karmic habit patterns get short-circuited, at least for a moment. Space appears. If the feeling continues, after the initial paralysis or shock, you become more porous, more alive and responsive, more connected to time and flows of energy and wisdom. You become more intelligent.

Medicine Three

A student once described the method of teaching in this tradition as sitting in front of an open fire hydrant. You are not fed little bite-sized morsels of teachings. You get Big View from the beginning. The vastness of the View itself can be like being shot into open space. You may find yourself participating in long hours of teachings. You may find yourself on retreat in close and even uncomfortable quarters with other students. You may be asked to work so hard that you literally don't have time to keep recreating your defensive, small self. Your teacher may deliberately provoke upsurges of emotion in you that you've been trying to contain with your various strategies and karmic scaffolding. You will find that your teacher is *not* relating to you in a way that can be predicted, and that she is impervious to your pleas for her to behave in a reasonable, noncontradictory, comfortable way.

Words of my Perfect Teacher is a documentary film by Leslie Ann Patton, a student of Dzongsar Khyentse Rinpoche. It's a wry, funny portrait of the play of the teacher-student relationship. At one point, Rinpoche tells the student who is narrating and directing the film that he's going to Bhutan, and he wants her to come with him. She gets all excited. Teacher wants me to go with him to Bhutan! She buys the ticket. She plans everything and waits expectantly for the day of departure.

A week before they're scheduled to leave, Rinpoche has one of his other students call her on the phone and announce, without any explanation, that the trip has been canceled. Rinpoche doesn't even call her himself. She is just left to deal with her outrage and feelings of disappointment, abandonment, and so on. As one of the other students in the movie says, if a friend does something you don't like, you can just ditch the friend, but if you've recognized that this is the teacher you want to be with for your whole life, or maybe even lifetimes, you are forced to deal with yourself. More importantly, you learn to open your heart and find wisdom even in the circumstances you considered to be upsetting. *You begin to notice that wisdom is working with you.*

In order to work in this way with a teacher, you have to understand what's happening. When students do not have an innate understanding of the direct-realization style of teacher-student relationship, they waste energy insisting that the teacher behave differently or apologize for having been somewhat upsetting. In other words, they try to force the teacher to relate on the ordinary terms set by the students.

But if you do understand, you can relax very deeply. Slowly, through this process, all the staleness of your life begins to melt away. You begin to relate directly and skillfully to the energy and wisdom of the moment. You become adaptable, playful, and expressive. When a spiritual teacher pushes small self to fall apart, it is difficult, but in a way that the teacher thinks you have the capacity to handle. The teacher is saying, "Be your extraordinary self; be your enlightened self for this moment." The teacher is expressing confidence that you can do that.

Your normal ways of dealing with yourself and life are extremely limited and constrained, fundamentally because you do not fully realize and cannot fully utilize your continuity with life. Your patterns of maintaining an experience of separation are habitual. They don't relate precisely, or at all, to interbeingness, to livingness. They are unspontaneous and scripted. They have you enslaved. Feeling overwhelmed, being forced to open to your environment and other people, being forced to ask for help, being forced to acknowledge the importance of alliances—this is great, great medicine. It's the spoonful of medicine that doesn't have the sugar in it. The sugar comes later, when the medicine has done its work.

MEDICINE FOUR

Feeling the loneliness that comes from maintaining a conceptual relationship to life

Medicine Four

Many of us are isolated behind a wall of stale ideas, thoughts, theories, and projections. We lose ourselves in habitual fantasies and fears about our relationships with other people. We have bought into the belief that being able to explain things demonstrates knowledge. We are continually trying to come up with packages of explanations. We keep the explanations hanging around, and we drag them out whenever we think they apply. The number one result of this mode of relating to life is loneliness.

When we're living through our conceptual mind, through our intellect and habitual emotional patterns, we feel lonely, but often we barely acknowledge it. We are living in this fantasy that we are being successful at projecting whatever we're projecting, explaining whatever it is we're explaining, coming up with our little analysis of everything. But talking at people and selling an image are not intimacy. Maybe we get some approval. Maybe we feel more accomplished than some other people. Maybe we get to hide out in stories about ourselves. But all the while, we're avoiding acknowledging our fundamental loneliness.

You cannot realize if you cannot experience the reality of your root loneliness. Our feeling of separation is the original, or initiating karma. It gives rise to all defensiveness, aggression and so on. Recognizing both the condition of feeling separate and its profound effects gives us the motivation to seek continuity.

I felt intensely lonely during my childhood and young adulthood. At the same time, I experienced a deep, abiding yearning for an unknown person or phenomenon I called "the Friend." I didn't feel satisfied spending time with friends who were not the Friend. I often didn't socialize because it left me yearning even more for the Friend. Of course, this is very dualistic, but that was my condition.

I wrote this poem when I was about 14 years old.

If I found you, my Friend
inside, you would find
only a tongue with no feathers
and nothing to say.
This time was not wasted but
going around
flooding and filling itself until now
there is nothing left but a silence
that is not yet not.

This poem expressed my feeling that without the Friend, life was too ordinary. I was becoming worn out by ordinariness. If I didn't find the Friend in time, my mouth would hold only a tongue. That tongue, and my words, would no longer be adorned with "feathers," meaning the colorful, magical quality of existence. It would have nothing to say if there was no response to my call, no one with whom to share the magic. Of course, we all seek to end loneliness through our ordinary relationships with others. But at some point, we recognize that no specific other is going to ameliorate our loneliness. Only self-realization can lead us to the recognition that the Friend is everywhere.

I was motivated by loneliness. And loneliness slowly opened me to compassion for others. I found it to be a great teacher. When I started to teach at University, I was deep into my sadhana. I began to feel directly that the conceptual way of relating to things was in my way as a teacher and in all of my relations with others. Professors are rewarded for shopping a kind of uber-confident, self-referential performance to their students. I realized this was not what I wanted to keep doing, but I couldn't imagine an alternative to performing a version of myself as the smart, funny, knowledgeable One. But once I became more aware of how the performance was contrived and feeding the experience of separation, it started to slip away naturally.

On the other side of the performance of small self, I discovered something surprising: actual intimacy with my students. I found myself relating to my students in a more raw and spontaneous way. I no longer just projected some knowledge or personality at them. This opened up a whole new space for connection, communication, and improvisation. Life began to feel more seamless and nourishing and fun.

Immediacy has been the hallmark of my experience since I abandoned trying to corral life with conceptual mind. These days, I feel that my senses, including my mind, are this huge open window, and you all are right here with me in blazing technicolor. I can feel directly the continuity of all that exists. To my utter astonishment, I don't feel lonely anymore. However, I couldn't have gotten here if I hadn't been willing to just feel lonely without trying to distract myself from that. Loneliness, the experience of separation itself, if you are willing to feel it, eventually brings you back to others. We can identify and become more porous to others through the shared experience of loneliness. Even now, the memory of that painful condition shines with beauty and poignancy.

MEDICINE FIVE

Feeling exhausted by your own striving

Many people in our culture experience a constant hum of anxiety about achievement. "Am I measuring up?" "Am I good enough?" "Am I clever enough?" You can probably feel it right now. All of this striving to be measured, to be great, to be admired, creates incredible, pervasive root exhaustion. Eventually exhaustion becomes so constant that you mistake it for a normal condition.

Over-striving, or sick effort, relates to the conviction that your self-worth is tied to recognizable, external achievements. Here in the u.s., nearly everyone strives to publicly achieve. We are not okay with simply being kind, good-hearted people who live, pray, work in the background, have some friends and maybe some family, and call it a life. We feel unfulfilled if we don't have a mission to achieve "more." I have never met a single u.s.-born person who did not experience some degree of this anxiety about achieving, accumulating achievements, and being recognized for doing so by other people.

Life requires effort at times. Life requires aggression at times. Life requires everything that life offers at some time or another. If I love something, and I am working hard at it, or I am doing something out of natural compassion, I can put out incredible effort, and it will be wonderful. That kind of effort is tiring in an ordinary way, but it will not make you sick. When you are operating more from the heart, you are drawing on a much bigger pool of energy. In contrast, when you are working hard, or doing strenuous sadhana in order to support self-image, that is sick effort. And sick effort really will make you ill.

Recently, the child of one of my students said, "I want to be a famous soccer player." When I was hanging out with arty types in my twenties, somebody would say, "I want to be a great writer," or "I want to be a great actor." I have heard people express the desire to be a great yogi, or a Guru. These statements are all rooted in an unhealthy need to achieve a certain self-image. Self-image is the real product. This kind of effort undermines actual enjoyment of our activities. Or it can prevent us from acting for fear of making mistakes, or for fear of the judgment of others, or for fear that others will unmask us and reveal that our greatness is nothing but fantasy.

If you sit down to write thinking that your goal is to be a great writer, you've already shot yourself in both feet. You're creating an incredible amount of tension. The artificiality and inauthenticity of the situation will cause you to write in an artificial, inauthentic way, if you can bear to write at all! You will sit down and try to imitate great writing. You won't actually have the patience, or the modesty, or the love for what you're doing to work day by day to develop your writing. You will feel, "I have to sit down and write something great from day one." You will cast about in your mind, "What does great writing sound like and look like?" Then you'll end up with a bunch of inauthentic stuff on the page.

The same thing applies to the rest of your life. If your goal in any area of your life is to be recognized for what you're doing, to be measured as successful and great at something, then you will always be projecting your internal image of what greatness looks like rather than actually living and expressing yourself. If you are just projecting an internal image of your idea of greatness, then you aren't actually great. It's a lose-lose situation.

When you are striving to be seen as great, you eventually become so exhausted that when no one is looking, you cheat and cut corners and fall apart. Your condition reveals itself in private. You strive to be great when someone is looking, and the rest of the time you are just too tired to even bother trying. Your greatness is very uneven! As you continue to grow more exhausted, you can lose affect. You find that you just don't care anymore, or you feel a kind of numbness or meaninglessness about your life. If you are lucky, this medicine can cause you to re-examine how you are living and inspire you to make some changes.

Certain people will adopt a spiritual persona, or will practice in a way that is designed to be noticed and earn kudos of some sort. They will get fancy "spiritual" tattoos, or wear "spiritual" clothing and accessories. They may talk in a "spiritual" way. Perhaps they appear in the eyes of some to be incredibly hard-working, dedicated yogis. Maybe they *are* hard-working, dedicated yogis! Of course, it is wonderful to act with thoroughness and dedication. It feels wonderful. But many people want their actions to be seen and measured. For instance, they offer help to someone, but they have the compulsion to tell somebody else about it. All of this just creates more and more exhaustion.

Competitiveness can infect entire cultures of spiritual traditions and communities. One of the communities in which I've been involved is very much like that. Theirs is a beautiful tradition, and I love the teacher, but the community is just riven with fantasies of spiritual superiority. Many of us desperately want to feel superior. But this attitude delays our spiritual progress. It also may detour the spiritual progress of others, or cause them to miss opportunities.

If you are teaching in a lineage, and you are being competitive and haughty, you will likely deter someone else from continuing with the stream of teachings you supposedly represent. That is really not a good situation.

Many people in yogic or direct realization traditions really do have a lot of energy. They are not easily exhausted. For them in particular, long-term over-striving can provoke a kind of bottoming out. They unexpectedly experience breakdown, or failure, or illness. Then they are confronted with the pride they have invested in being strong. This can lead to the recognition that they have to change their approach to sadhana. It can lead to true modesty and appreciation for impermanence. Utter exhaustion can be the moment when you recognize that you have to find a different way of being in the world. It can bring more softness and more openness and more honesty.

There is a book of advice that Padmasambhava, the second Buddha, gave to his disciple, Yeshe Tsogyal. One of the things he told her has stuck in my mind and has been so important in my own practice. He said to her, "Don't meditate on or fabricate even as much as an atom."[18] When we are doing sadhana, any fantasy about ourselves is *not* sadhana. Fantasy will not wake you up. You simply cannot get there if you are engaged in any kind of fantasy. There's no fantasy that you can get away with. There's no fantasy that you can hold onto. And fantasies about being a great practitioner, or being in a superior spiritual tradition are fantastically popular! Whatever fantasy you are engaging in about yourself or your tradition is 110 percent blocking your path. Try to use "don't fabricate even as much as an atom" as a guide.

Sick effort represents a level of fantasy. Part of the fantasy is that you are in control of the results of your practice. Another fantasy is that you are great, dedicated, more hardcore, or more sincere than others. You might be putting in a lot of time on the cushion, but you are wasting whatever percentage of your effort is in the service of appearing a certain way. That is very ordinary, karmic effort. It's the same old, same old, but in some sort of spiritual guise. You need to acknowledge that and let go of striving to be recognized as being a good practitioner or disciple. Uncompromising honesty is actually the siddhi that you, and all of us, need.

On the other hand, we are all mixed bags. No one is 100 percent sincere or 100 percent lacking in fantasy. But we all have some degree of sincerity, and we can try our best to adhere to that. As we make that effort, the Mother in her wisdom gives us circumstances in our practice and in our lives that strip us of fantasy, that strip us of the attachment to unhealthy striving. I can think of any numbers of situations in my life where this occurred.

I inherited one particularly strong fantasy concept from some of my spiritual teachers, and from my culture: we should always try to grow our influence. Many of us take this as natural or a given. But if you think about it for a moment, the equation of growth with success is just another concept. There is no necessary connection between the two. In fact, not every circumstance calls for growth, and sometimes things work out best when we withdraw or downsize. The most opportunity always comes from simply offering your gifts and letting go. When I say "opportunity," I mean opportunity to realize.

When I first moved to Portland, Oregon and started teaching, I was still blinded by my attachment to growing Jaya Kula into a big and well-known organization. Most of my teachers had tried to do this with their own organizations, and I had bought into the idea that getting large was desirable in and of itself. I rented an 800-square-foot yoga studio in order to hold a weekly satsang based on the teachings of Anandamayi Ma. I bought a huge urn for chai, a case of paper cups, and large amounts of other supplies. I made posters and hung them all around town.

The first inkling that things would not go as planned came through talking to the people managing the shops and yoga studios where I was hanging posters. Not a single person I met had ever heard of Anandamayi Ma. In my fantasy projection, she was famous, and people would naturally be terribly excited about studying her teachings! Then, some people did show up to the satsang, but definitely not in the numbers I had projected. I had one fantasy, and reality met me differently.

Around this time, I went to get a divination from a Tibetan yogini I knew. I asked her about Jaya Kula and whether it would be successful. She moved the beads across her fingers and chanted the mantras. Then she looked up at me and said, "mediocre." She moved the beads, divining once more and added the comment, "low mediocre."

I must have looked crestfallen. She gazed at me with a complex expression of compassion and mockery. "When you want to help sentient beings, you must expect obstacles," she admonished me. I count this as one of the most wonderful teachings I have ever received. It helped me to learn patience, perseverance, adaptability, and to remain heart-centered no matter what. The yogini reminded me that my desire to be of use, not the karmic compulsion to grow and be recognized, should remain front and center.

After that, I donated the urn to the local Tibet center. I started holding satsang in the living room of my apartment. Some evenings, only three people would show up. Within a few years, the core of our community was established. The case of paper cups I had purchased at the beginning of our journey lasted for about ten years. After this, and many other experiences, it is a source of wonder to me that I feel totally content just offering the teachings without making any effort to grow. In fact, I now feel a little afraid about getting too large!

Our culture rewards type-A behaviors. It rewards sick effort. This makes it doubly hard to tear yourself away from those fantasies. But please understand that if you really want to wake up, if

Medicine Five

you really want to know what's going on here and who you are, you can't take the greatness fantasy with you. You don't get to indulge the greatness thing. You don't get to keep your self-image and your immodesty. Even if you don't have a teacher who can see what you're doing, at least you know that primordial wisdom is seeing everything you're doing. Thinking you're getting away with anything is just a joke.

The truth of your existence is that you are equally as valuable as anybody else, no matter what you do. No matter how many mistakes you make, or how small or great your accomplishments are, your value never changes. It's not dependent on how you are showing up, or how you are performing. You have the same indestructible Vajra nature as everyone else.

MEDICINE SIX

Finding your usual pleasures to be hollow and boring

Medicine Six is about finally growing tired of your habits. You begin to experience well-worn pleasures as tasteless, tawdry, gross, hollow, or boring. You begin to experience the limitations of what you previously avidly pursued. You might think, "Yay!" But going through this can feel quite destabilizing at first until you get the hang of it.

When I was growing up in the 1950s and 60s, no one in my family had ever eaten yogurt. Yogurt was not yet a big thing in the U.S. When I hit age twelve or thirteen, my family discovered Dannon yogurt. It was full of sugar and highly processed, but to us Dannon was the epitome of healthy. The yogurt was thoroughly blended with sugar and some sort of preserves. It had this smell vaguely like Play-Doh, and it was artificially glossy. Most likely, it was diet Dannon. Everything in our house had artificial sweetener in it.

Eventually, ignorance started to lift. Dannon introduced yogurt that you mixed yourself. This was supposed to be healthier than pre-blended yogurt, because, you know, D.I.Y. It had a bit of preserves on the bottom, and on the top was just yogurt. I believe that the container came with a little wooden spoon for stirring. Stirring by hand encouraged us to feel "Thank God we're not eating that pre-blended stuff anymore!"

Then came the advent of yogurt made with organic, pasteurized milk. A little later, we started to have a proliferation of yogurt choices: goat milk yogurt, soy milk yogurt, sheep milk yogurt, Greek yogurt, coconut milk yogurt, all these different kinds of yogurts.

Around 2010, we arrive at grass-fed organic yogurt. Now we think we have reached the pinnacle of yogurt. I wouldn't touch the blended yogurt that I was given when I was a kid, or the yogurt you stir from the bottom that I previously thought was so healthy, or the merely organic yogurt. Poison! Now it's all about the grass-fed organic yogurt. Until I moved to Maine.

It's 2013. The grass-fed organic yogurt that they sell in Whole Foods is pasteurized. Can you believe that? And it is not local. QED: it's poison. Now I have to have my local, grass-fed organic raw milk yogurt. The best! Finally, I've reached the nirvana of the yogurt world. All other yogurts now taste terrible to me, or I just feel revulsion when I eat them, even if they taste good, because I know they're poison. I am armed with all of this information about my intestinal flora. Do you think it ends here? No.

Thanks to one of my students, I discover the hot box—a wonderful device for proofing bread and fermenting. Now I buy my raw milk, widely available in Maine, from only one farm. The milk comes from Jersey cows, and it just looks better than all the other raw, organic, grass-fed, pasture-raised local milks. I must get it on the day it's delivered so that it has been out of the cow for fewer than twenty-four hours. The yogurt must be made immediately, *and* it has to be twelve-hour fermented yogurt made with a special, mail order lactobacillus starter. The resulting yogurt must be eaten within two days, because after that, the good bacteria start to die off. I suppose the next step is owning the cow, although, laziness may get in the way there a little!

This same process is happening to you as you practice. Many pleasures you formerly enjoyed will at some point taste like the blended, artificially-sweetened yogurt I ate back in 1970. Day-by-day, pleasures that are unsubtle, gross, limited, and essentially not an expression of the full-on sweetness of life, are going to seem hollow and boring. You will start to desire pleasures that express more of life's intelligence, nuanced artistry, and unadulterated goodness.

You will definitely notice more acutely the compulsion fueling your own relationships and those of others. Relationships based largely on karmic habits will begin to feel artificial and limiting, just like aspartame-sweetened Dannon yogurt. Perhaps you will stop listening to tortured love songs because you will now experience the sentiments they express as being the products of profound limitation. You will feel *more* compassion for the suffering that people experience in their relationships, but you're not going to be identified with those patterns anymore.

Student: Okay, but aren't we supposed to end up with the capacity to enjoy *everything*? I remember when I was in India, I'd go to someone's house, and they're serving Fanta. I didn't want to drink it! I can get so precious about what I want and what I don't want, as opposed to what's in front of me. But this isn't ideal, right?

Shambhavi: When we're at somebody's house and they're serving us, even if it's crappy food, we're not going to be rude. We're going to eat it, unless we have to say we're allergic to something. If it's not a deadly allergy, we might still eat it.

In India where people are serving really spicy food, or they're serving gluten, which I'm allergic to, or Fanta, or whatever they're serving, I'm generally going to eat it. I want to be generous to my hosts by appreciating their hospitality. I might even get sick. That's okay up to a point. But we choose differently if we have the option to feed ourselves. By "feed," I mean in the largest sense of taking in our circumstances, our relationships, our work, our spiritual practice, our actual literal food, what we read, and what media we enjoy.

Medicine Six

When we begin to wake up, we experience a natural desire and a natural capacity to feed ourselves according to what is good for a human being. We develop a natural desire to stop "eating" anything that will hamper our practice and our lives.

When we talk about self-realization and enjoying everything, we mean appreciating everything without exception as an expression of the supreme reality. It doesn't mean that we ignore our relative experience and toss out our discernment. Even realized people decide what to eat and with whom to spend their time.

We eat unhealthily a lot of the time. When we make such choices as a matter of habit, we are expressing our limitation. In Ayurveda, when we eat wrongly or live in a way that is not good for our constitution, that is called *prajñaparadha*, or a crime against wisdom. We even find such "crimes" exciting because, on some level, compulsion has a kind of intensity that can be pleasurable. The pattern of repeatedly craving and then satisfying a craving is also pleasurable.

If we are practicing, those attachments start to fall away naturally. The first thing that falls away, before we actually get out of a circumstance, is the compulsion to repeat. We go through a period of time when the compulsion is resolving, or dissolving, and we're losing interest in whatever it was we were compulsive about. We don't need our intensity fix anymore, or our crave-and-binge fix. It has resolved, but nothing has yet come to take its place. So we experience a weird kind of neutrality, or hollowness, or boredom.

As we're waking up, we go through periods during which we're not as excited about life as we used to be. I just went through this with espresso. Up until recently, if I knew that every day I could get up and have espresso, I would experience a happy feeling and a craving. I never could drink espresso every day because my health would have been terrible. But I definitely had this feeling of compulsion. Eventually, after decades, it went away.

Now when I think about having espresso, I just don't care. And even if I do happen to drink espresso, I barely notice that I'm drinking it. It's kind of disappointing. I just feel blah and neutral about espresso now. That's an expression of the interim period. I'm in a *bardo*, or gap, during which the compulsion is fading, and the wider View or bigger experience has not quite arrived.

The hallmark of the resolution of karma is that you cannot manufacture that compulsion again. You can think of it, but you can't recall it experientially. When you are still in the grip of compulsions, it's very easy to call them up and sort of activate them on purpose. But when the karma is resolving, and you're in one of these real bardos, you cannot get back to it. I can tell you the story about how I felt about espresso, but I cannot feel it again. I just can't. I've been trying, but it's now just another drink to me.

When your senses are tied up in compulsion, they're limited. It's like driving through a tunnel rather than walking through a big open field. You're in a dark tunnel, and it's very exciting because you're speeding along, but you really can't see that much, or experience much other than sort of an adrenaline rush. But if you're walking through a big field, your senses are more relaxed and open. You are experiencing a lot more. On the other side of that speeding tunnel of compulsion is a more relaxed and rich liveliness.

Understand that the feeling of neutrality, or blah, or disinterestedness toward something you used to enjoy, is a bardo, a transition. Karma is being released. You need to surf the bardo by continuing to do your practice, and you will eventually discover more clarity and a more nuanced appreciation for the diversity of life.

MEDICINE SEVEN

Recognizing the wisdom in pain and fear

Before I talk about recognizing the wisdom in pain and fear, I want to talk about something that has to happen first. You have to actually recognize that you're in pain and afraid. A person who shoots heroin generally knows that they're afraid and in pain. They won't deny it. Heroin addicts are more honest than many of us. Most of us lie about our condition to ourselves and others. We interpret fear or pain of any sort, even just being sick in an ordinary way, as a personal failure that we want to hide from other people. Sometimes we even get defensive and angry if a friend says sympathetically, "You look tired." Even ordinary tiredness can be an affront to our pride.

The avoidance of recognizing our own pain and fear is the origin of spiritual bypassing, aka using spiritual teachings to mask our fear of death. I am talking right now about recognizing the wisdom in pain and fear. When this talk is finished, one of you might use this teaching to avoid actually feeling any fear and pain. For instance, a friend notices your pain, and you might take up a defensive stance by replying in a knowing tone of voice, "There is wisdom in pain." But you're not feeling your pain. You are avoiding it.

Even highly realized people get tired, feel pain, fall ill, and die. Ramana Maharshi died of cancer, and so did the 16th Karmapa. The Dalai Lama has been in the hospital numerous times. I've heard that Amma has diabetes. Go around spouting *eka rasa* all you want; you're still going to get sick, and you are going to go through times when you are tired and weak and in pain.

After more than three decades of daily sadhana, I do have the experience of more enjoyment and more appreciation for the variety of people and circumstances I encounter. I'm able to feel love and compassion for people, regardless of what condition they're in. I am not so afraid of pain or dying. But if I eat moldy food, I'm still going to get sick. None of us are going to be able to digest everything that life serves up. We have to be real in order to receive real wisdom.

One time in India I got dengue fever. I didn't know that I had it, but somebody invited me over to their house just as the fever was blazing high. My hosts had cooked a beautiful meal full of spices and gluten. I was practically keeling over, and I was trying to eat it to be polite. Eventually I just said, "I can't. I'm too sick." So, we all have limitations, and every situation is unique. We always have to be humble and live to our real circumstances.

If you want to discover the wisdom in fear and pain, you first must *feel* fear and pain. You can't acknowledge these only in an intellectual way. You have to stop meddling with your fear and pain. You have to stop trying to ignore, minimize, deny, or cover up your fear and pain with various distractions and activities and substances. You must stop using spiritual teachings to try to convince yourself and other people that you are rising above pain, or that you are relating to fear in some spiritual way when you are not.

When I first started teaching, I discovered that many people are terrified of feeling afraid. Any little fear can cause an outsized secondary reaction of greater fear. If we feel a pain, or we're sick, we sometimes become very fearful. This reactivity emerges from living without acknowledging impermanence and the groundlessness of our lives. We try to ignore death, and we crave unreal imperviousness. Then we get into a situation in which we cannot tolerate even small reminders of our fragility. So we have this big overblown reaction to fear and pain.

Fear and pain are extremely useful situations for practitioners. They can yank us out of our normal, self-deluded, habitual ways of relating and feeling and thinking. If we allow it, they can cut through our karmic habit patterns, cut through our desensitization to life, cut through our stories about who we are, and bust open the hothouse of "me, myself, and I" in which we generally live.

Pain and fear can give us an opportunity to acknowledge that we are not in control of life. Something larger is at work. We can have the useful experience of not being able to handle everything. We learn about interdependency. We can acknowledge our fragility, our impermanence. We can learn about adapting. We can get to a point where we want to re-examine the fundamentals of our lives. We question what's really important to us. We can acknowledge the inauthenticity of how we have been living prior to experiencing this fear and pain.

Through fear and pain, we can find out about the ignorance, inauthenticity, and compulsion that have been driving our lives. We are forced to dig deeper and to discover more actual wisdom in ourselves and allies. That's how we mine, in an ordinary way, wisdom from fear and pain. It's actually our own, natural and inherent wisdom that we've been ignoring. We have all had this experience to some degree or another.

In a more subtle way, fear and pain are deliberately invoked in direct realization practice. These are not necessarily beginning practices, but they are a part of every tradition in which I have studied. Fear engenders a kind of shock that opens up the subtle channels and disables conceptual mind for at least a moment. Then we can practice in that relatively empty condition. So we sometimes use shocking mantras designed to cut through conceptual mind.

We might deliberately place ourselves in scary situations, such as practicing alone in the woods where there are wild animals, or in cremation grounds.

We can also do spiritual practice directly with the fear and pain that arise in the course of everyday life. If we find ourselves in a situation of pain or illness, or we're very afraid, and the ground seems to be dropping out of our world, we can deliberately invoke our practice in midst of this turmoil. But it's not just about waiting for some life event to pull the rug out from under us. We can use smaller moments of pain and fear, such as stubbing a toe, or a near-miss car accident, or someone yelling at us. We experience these small moments of pain and fear quite regularly. We can start to experiment with them as opportunities for spiritual practice. When we do mantra, or meditation, or kriya yoga, in these circumstances, we can resolve karma more quickly.

The best way to work with fear and pain in everyday life emerges from having an established meditation practice. I'm talking about when you actually have an experience of the meditative state. We call this the state of your practice. The idea of any sadhana or spiritual practice is not just to do some technique. Technique is just a vehicle. It's like a diving board. The diving board isn't diving; it's just the thing from which you jump. In the same way, the meditation technique is not meditating. Meditating is what reveals itself as a result of the technique. It's what the technique leads you into.

If you have a solid recognition of the state of your practice, then when you feel any kind of disturbance, you remember to drop into that condition right then and there. You just bring on the state of your practice, and you see what happens. This is a profound and powerful act. I'm not going to tell you what happens, but it will change your whole relationship to pain and fear if you do this. Try it as an experiment and see.

You can also turn pain and fear into sadhana by doing what we call Guru Yoga. In Dzogchen and Trika Shaivism there are many forms of Guru Yoga. Guru Yoga is based on the understanding that you and your Guru, or you and the Guru principle in the cosmic sense, share the same enlightened essence nature. Your enlightened essence nature is obscured by karma, but only as the sun is obscured by clouds. By doing Guru Yoga, you can recognize your indestructible real nature in a direct, experiential way.

The simplest form of Guru Yoga can be practiced by anyone who has a feeling of connection to Guru, whether Guru be a living teacher, or someone such as Buddha or Padmasambhava or Anandamayi Ma. All you need to do is think of that person. You're in pain, or you're feeling fear, and you just start thinking of that person. Don't just think of them once. You need to think of Guru continuously through the experience of pain or fear. You must consistently become aware of that being and try to connect with them. Then, if you have an authentic connection to that Guru, you will have a similar kind of effect as when you drop into the state of your meditation practice.

Ultimately, through our practice and direct experience of reality, we come to understand that all circumstances are made of wisdom. Our job is to use our minds and our other senses to directly perceive that. Then we can work in the best possible way with circumstance. Being in the state of our practice means that our senses are relaxed and receptive. We can contact and receive wisdom more easily. It doesn't mean that we are numbing out or doing an end run around our fear and pain. We are just trying to contact wisdom and be immersed in that.

When you are practicing with little pains and little fears, you are trying to develop a proper relationship with pain and fear. Your responses to pain and fear become more practical, honest, and non-hysterical. Don't do the pop psychological thing where you "go into it," and the pain or fear becomes your whole world. You're not trying to do that. You want pain and fear to take up only an appropriate plot in the landscape of your life. Doing Guru Yoga or being in the state of your meditation practice is about finding that appropriate relationship. You are relating to pain and fear in a simple, straight-forward, practical, and practitioner-like way with no extra bells and whistles. Then you can apprehend and appreciate the wisdom.

I used to be extremely afraid of flying. I was about fifteen years old, and not yet a practitioner, when this started. My earlier way of dealing with it was basically valium and alcohol. But I wised up eventually when I started practicing non-conceptual, open-eyed meditation. One time, I was on a plane, and I just started prac-ticing this way. You have no idea how hard that was. When you drop into non-conceptual meditation, you are utterly defenseless. The fear raced through my body like a powerful cheetah. But I held my ground. When the fear distracted me, I returned to meditation. Then I discovered a whole other aspect of this situation that could only appear when I was not trying to drown out the fear or defend myself, when I was open with the fear, in spite of the fear, or per-haps because of the fear.

Basically, I saw God. I don't mean that some figure appeared to me, but I was completely immersed in the groundless natural state. I learned so much from this. After that, I couldn't wait to get on the plane and be terrified! Most of us do not get the opportunity to feel terror on a regular basis. I suddenly felt extremely lucky to have this fear. Unfortunately, now I'm no longer afraid of flying!

MEDICINE EIGHT

Realizing that waking life is like a painting, a drama, or a dream

This medicine is bitter in the beginning and sweet in the finish. The bitter taste comes from recognizing that your life, your world, and *all* worlds simply do not exist precisely in the way you currently assume they do. The happenstances of your life do not carry the weight of importance you currently give to them. If you continue to practice, you will be called upon to give up your feeling of urgency about life. In fact, in the face of the revelation of the real nature of things, you will discover that life is both a drama and a play of experience. Experiences are what exist, not things. Bitter taste is a tonic that cools emotions and aids digestion. With the help of this bitter medicine, you will eventually be able to taste the profound sweetness of existence itself.

In many spiritual traditions, particularly those from India and Tibet, students receive the teaching that this life is like a dream. Students, and even some teachers, often interpret this to mean that everything we are and experience is unreal, or even that we ourselves and manifest life do not exist. People studying Patanjali's

Yoga Sutras in yoga classes and in yoga teacher trainings in the U.S., also often receive the teaching that life is an illusion. Some teachers and traditions have a more sophisticated understanding of this teaching, but by the time the teaching filters down to the average person, it devolves into a cloudy idea that everything is unreal. The number one thing that I want you to try to remember is that just because our everyday world is like a painting, a drama, or a dream, does not mean it is unreal. Paintings are real paintings. Dramas are real dramas. And dreams are real dreams.

This idea about ordinary life being unreal has been around for centuries in India. More nuanced teachings from the Vedantic tradition point to mistaken perceptions rather than the unreality of the world in its entirety. You may recall the famous rope and snake parable. We can mistake a rope seen from a distance for a snake, but that does not make the rope unreal. As we draw nearer and can see more clearly, the illusion of the snake is revealed and the rope appears. At the same time, our experience of the snake was also a real illusion and a real experience. Nowhere is there ground for an argument for absolute unreality. But it is quite astounding how students, teachers, and whole traditions have reduced this more nuanced View to the nonsensical claim that manifest life is unreal and does not exist.

The founders of what we now call Trika Shaivism pointed to what may be the crux of the distinction between the View of Trika Shaivism and many other spiritual traditions from the Indian subcontinent. They argued that the unreal cannot exist. Nonexistence cannot exist. This almost seems like a trick, but it isn't. It is an insurmountable argument against the claim that anything is unreal. Furthermore, if you divide phenomena or experience into the real and the unreal, or the real and the illusory, you are reintroducing dualism. Some Advaita Vedantins pride themselves on being the most thorough-going nondualists. But by dismissing things as unreal, they trap themselves into an unsolvable paradox.[19]

Most people, in my experience, don't understand what it means to say things are unreal. They sort of nod along, thinking "oh yes, things are unreal," but they don't know what it means. Because it can't actually mean anything. And if you think about it, if you think about existence itself, there cannot be anything unreal in existence itself. *Everything is real.* Of course, this doesn't mean that things are as you assume they are. Your experience of things and your View of things may be mistaken or incomplete. But that doesn't make your experience unreal. All experiences are real experiences. A mistaken idea is a real idea. An overreaction is a real emotion.

From an ordinary, scientific perspective, your body is made of atoms and subatomic particles and space. In fact, you are actually mostly empty space. But you have the real experience of being a solid body. If, however, you form the idea that your body is solid, based on your superficial experience, that is an incomplete View. Again, it is a *real* experience, but it is not a complete experience or a complete View. The fact that the experience of having a solid body is being produced somehow by atoms whirling in space is fantastic and magical. Appreciation for the "illusion," or glamour of the creation, is a hallmark of Trika Shaivism and other direct realization traditions.

In Western cultures, we have divided the world up into what is real and material and what is imaginary, or mental, or spiritual. In Trika Shaivism, we make no such divisions. We actually practice dropping those conceptual divisions in order to be able to perceive the real nature of all phenomena. From the perspective of Trika, all phenomena are real expressions of the same Self. They are expressions of one, continuous, all pervading consciousness and its energy. All experiences—of solidity, of individuality, of people, beings, and worlds—are produced by, of, and within this Self. What this Self produces *are* experiences. It does not produce bodies; it produces experiences of bodies. It does not produce matter; it produces experiences of matter. There is an exact continuum here between atoms swirling in space producing the experience of a solid body, and God producing all experiences of form out of consciousness and energy. But make no mistake, scientific observation does not explain or verify yoga or yogic cosmology. What we observe from an ordinary, scientific perspective are expressions being produced within and by the pervasive Self.

Through our direct experience as practitioners, we come to realize that reality works the same way all the way down. Atoms in space producing the experience of solidity are an expression, or echo, of the entire cosmic process of Self-expression. At a more subtle level, when your inner eyes open, you can see subtle atoms. These are called *bindu* in Sanskrit and *thigles* in Tibetan. These bindu sit behind and produce experiences such as atoms. But there are even more subtle expressions sitting behind and producing bindu. Ultimately, there is only consciousness and energy from which all experience emerges.

When you are dreaming, you experience dream objects as if they are solid, and you experience dream emotions as if they are appropriate to the circumstance. You are dreaming of driving a car. You experience the car as having solidity. Your hand is on a solid steering wheel. When you see a crash coming, you feel fear. If you think about it, you are making the same assumptions in your dreams that you are making in this life. You assume the dream car is solid, but it is made of awareness and the creative energy of awareness. Likewise, in your everyday life, you assume that your body and your world are solid, but they are made of tiny atoms and a whole lot of space. You assume that you and your world are made up of separate objects, but all objects are made of consciousness and energy and are continuous, experiential events.

The power to produce the infinitely diverse experiences of people, beings, and worlds is called *Maya*. The essence of the distinction between Trika and other nondual traditions from India can be understood by exploring this one word. In many scriptures and

119

Medicine Eight

spiritual teaching texts from India, Maya is translated as "illusion" and is denigrated as a powerful, negative force. In Trika Shaivism, Maya is a great Devi, a great Shakti, and is revered. Maya is the Shakti who creates the infinity of diverse experiences and forms.[20] In the Trika tradition, and also in the Shakta Tantrik tradition of Bengal, this power is said to be Lord Shiva's magic or glamour. The world of name and form is celebrated as a great festival. Rather than being maligned, it is appreciated as a multi-faceted jeweled ornament, or a great city, to which one travels and experiences diverse displays of creativity.[21]

When the teachings say that our experience, or this life, is like a dream, or a painting, or a play, they are saying that consciousness and its energy are causing this colorful display to appear out of itself, of itself. They are also saying that manifest life is a creative expression of the Supreme Self and has the value of a work of art. So another thing we need to understand about this medicine is that, ultimately, we are not feeling depressed about life being like a dream, or a painting, or a play. Dreams are fun and fantastical. We enjoy paintings and plays. We are not exclaiming, "Oh it's *just* a dream," or "It's *just* a painting!" or "It's *just* a play!" We may be upset or disappointed at first, but eventually we become happy about this state of affairs.

The question of suffering and evil always arises in the context of dualistic, relative experience. Yet even in the Buddhist traditions, which we identify so much with teachings about suffering, the absolute, non-relative teaching is that there is no suffering,[22] there is no evil. This may shock you, but that is only a product of the fact that many contemporary schools and teachers of Buddhism in the West never get around to, or actually don't know, the absolute View of their own traditions.

I like to compare our experience of suffering and evil to the situation of soap opera actors. Presumably, actors in soap operas enjoy playing their histrionic roles. But what if they forget that they are actors? Suddenly, the myriad affairs, divorces, deaths, and other disasters cease to be enjoyable. The suffering feels very real. We are like those actors. Our real nature is God, and God is playing all of the roles. God is even playing the role of the actor who has forgotten that this is a play of consciousness and its energy.

We can enjoy a painting of a terrible event, say Picasso's famous *Guernica* that depicts chaos and suffering during wartime. In general, when we see a painting of war, we don't have the same reaction to it as we would if we were standing in the middle of a battlefield. We understand that it's a painting. At the same time, we may feel many emotions while experiencing a work of art. We cry and laugh, and feel love, and desire, and anger, and compassion, and even envy and humiliation. Even when we recognize that life is like a painting, or a dream, or a drama, we still feel a wide range of emotions, but we are not so identified with them or disturbed by them. In fact, in the context of experiencing a work of art, we enjoy our emotions.

We go to the movies and experience terrible things and enjoy them. We enjoy crying at the movies and feeling scared. We even enjoy movies about entire continents and worlds being destroyed. Maybe you are concerned about the destruction of the environment. It is totally natural to feel concern. It is totally natural to want to stop the destruction. And it is also totally natural to destroy. If this upsets you, I really urge you to consider why we enjoy big disaster movies. This is not a glib question; it's a very deep question.

We sit there and watch the planet literally crumble to bits, laughing our heads off. The entire West Coast falls off into the ocean, and we feel thrilled and can't wait to see even more destruction. Then the next day, we are marching around with signs that say, "Save the West Coast!" You really have to ask yourself why this is. Dualistic View cannot explain why we love disaster movies, why we love seeing things blown up, why we love movies about terrorists, why we love movies about failed romance and children dying of cancer and all kinds of things that traumatize us in everyday life.

121

Medicine Eight

We spend an absolutely enormous percentage of our time telling stories, creating story media, and consuming story media. Why do we do this? Think about it. Things could always be otherwise. Isn't it at least a bit strange that from childhood to death, we are such relentless story makers and story enjoyers? If you have a dualistic View, you cannot explain why we continually generate all this creative material about things that are so upsetting to us. If bad relationships and loss and death are actually terrible in the objective way we believe them to be, then why would we want to relive them on the screen and in novels and pop songs day after day?

The bitter medicine is learning that our lives and works of art are not different on the level of their origin and their real nature. Our world is basically God's cosmic movie studio, cosmic drama, cosmic dream. Our world, including all of our emotions, is ultimately to be enjoyed as a reflection of the wild creativity of an alive, aware Self. And when we retrace our steps and rediscover that living awareness permeates everything equally, the level of our suffering plummets.

The 16th Karmapa, when he was dying, gave this teaching in the best possible way. The Karmapa was beloved by the students of Chögyam Trungpa Rinpoche. He died in the u.s. of cancer, and many of Trungpa Rinpoche's students were involved in caring for him during his final days. One such student was sitting by the Karmapa's bedside in the hospital. He sobbed inconsolably, his head resting on the bed by the Karmapa's side. According to the student's own report, the Karmapa lay quietly, not saying anything. Eventually, this fellow lifted his head. The Karmapa looked at him with utmost compassion and said, "Nothing ever happens."[23]

When our attachment to dualistic View is cut, when we have perceived that our ordinary world is composed of a parade of experiences generated by consciousness and energy, then we understand that nothing ever happens in the way we ordinarily assume. Endless experiences of form are generated, but there are not really any substantial forms here. There are real experiences of substantiality.

There are real experiences of individuality, of plants and rivers, of birth and death, of wars, of murder and mayhem. Just as real light plays on a screen to generate the experience of a movie, the real light of consciousness shines forth to create the infinity of experiences of all that exists.

We are children of this alive, self-aware reality. We are made by and of that, and we reflect the real nature of that in our everyday lives, albeit in our more limited way. We are busy generating all of these narrative productions just as God is. When we make art, and tell and enjoy stories, we are expressing and enacting something central to the nature of reality.

I've gotten into trouble many times with this teaching. Someone inevitably feels upset or even outraged. We are very attached to our outrage. We are attached to our views about right and wrong, good and bad. So if someone comes along and says all experiences are like a play or a dream, that's a heinous teaching. Yet realizing this is at the heart of Self-realization.

Of course, our experiences don't all have the same taste, texture, smell, or emotional weight. We have access to an infinite variety of sensory experiences and circumstances. We really are living in this huge Costco of potential experiences. Emotions such as sorrow, anger, grief, and caring are all part of the expressive capacity of this reality. Self-realization is not bland. It is not unexpressive. It is not neutral. When you become more realized, you become more expressive, not less. You just aren't so attached to everything being a certain way.

Medicine Eight

MEDICINE NINE

Recognizing that you are always dissatisfied in the end

We all desire unbroken security and contentment. The little engine inside of us continually chugs along, looking for a final resolution to the problem of our fragile existence. We look for it in the supermarket. We look for it when we gather with friends. We look for it in our romantic relationships. We look for it in drugs and alcohol. We look for it while binge-watching TV shows. But eventually we can realize that impermanence does not offer us what we seek, so we look for it in spiritual practice.

When starting a spiritual practice, many people are still willing to settle for ordinary security and contentment. They want a break from their lives. They want to relax a little. They want to function better at their jobs, or as parents or friends. They want to achieve something that will make them feel great about themselves and be admired by others. The goal of achieving ordinary security and contentment is imported into the field of spiritual life, often because people have not yet recognized their capacity to enter into an extraordinary relationship with reality. Once they get a glimpse of the extraordinary, the more mundane results of spiritual practice become disappointing.

Anandamayi Ma taught that dissatisfaction with the impermanent keeps us searching for the eternal.[24] Getting what we want and then having it taken away, or just recognizing that whatever we seek in impermanence won't ultimately satisfy us, is one of the great game strategies in this natural process of waking up. A mere feeling of dissatisfaction is not sufficient, however. You also must recognize that what you thought was going to do it for you isn't going to do it for you. If you simply feel dissatisfied with donut A without any recognition, you will keep on trying with donuts B, C, and D. Many of us are temporarily stuck in this kind of repetitive, horizontal seeking.

We all have a built-in longing for the eternal and a built-in feeling of discomfort with our limited existence. Both longing and dissatisfaction are the voices of God urging us toward our real destination. As long as we're still in ordinary mind, we keep thinking, "Oh, if I just get a better boyfriend, or a better job, or a better donut, or a better house, or a better mantra, or more admiring friends… I'll be happy." If we are driven by these limited longings, spiritual awakening will also be limited, but we can still progress because we are being led by longing, and we will never fail to be dissatisfied in the end.

Longing and dissatisfaction can eventually lead us to look for an accomplished teacher, an openhearted community, and effective practices. Ultimately, we understand that the only thing that is going to totally resolve our anxiety is recognizing our real nature and experiencing our immersion in that.

Throughout most of our non-realized life, we experience the ordinary pulse between temporary satisfaction and dissatisfaction. Let's say you sit down to meditate for the first time. You feel some anxiety and discomfort. Then if you manage to keep sitting, at some point you feel a little more calm. You think, "Oh, this is good. I feel calm. I feel more relaxed." Then you go to work. You have a calmer day. But then if you keep sitting, on some days you don't feel better. You feel worse. You are holding the concept that having once experienced calmness, you will just keep improving, growing calmer still. But that doesn't happen. All of these emotions and sensations and thoughts start to manifest while you're sitting. You find out that you actually have to deal with yourself and how you are. You find out that meditation is not valium.

Many people decide beforehand what spiritual practice is for. It's for calming your mind. It's for learning how to be compassionate. It's for obtaining some special powers, controlling energy, or taking a light body. Whatever you decide at the outset is limited, no matter how rational or grand your goal may sound. Dissatisfaction keeps you from getting stuck. For the purpose of not getting stuck, no amount of dissatisfaction is too much! Even when you have big realizations, or openings, the dissatisfaction that inevitably arises again lets you know not to get attached. It tells you to keep going.

So even in our spiritual practice, the pulse between getting something we want and dissatisfaction is happening. And we eventually recognize that this pulse is an important aspect of practice. If we just remained on the surface, feeling content with being a little calmer, we would never find the desire and determination to realize. If we were content with controlling energy, we would never open our hearts. But fuller and fuller tastes of presence, punctuated by being kicked back to a relative experience of separation, inflame the desire to do more practice. Every incomplete move we make toward self-realization includes within it the seed of discontent that moves us to surrender more deeply.

Dissatisfaction is like a karmic dredging machine. It can drive us to do more practice. It can also piss us off and cause us to go on a spiritual strike for some period of time. In earlier stages of unfolding, when you feel dissatisfied and discontent, you're going to have all kinds of stories about why that is so. You're going to blame other people, or the state of the world. If you're lucky, you find a teacher. Then you can blame your teacher, or your practice. Maybe you will blame your psychology, or your astrology. Those stories are your karmas manifesting. If you can look and see the stories for what they are, you can begin to drop them and grow.

Ultimately, feeling discontent with our spiritual "attainments," or lack thereof, humbles us. It causes us to return to practice with a new dedication, a new commitment, a new sense of simply having to walk and put one foot in front of the other and deal with whatever comes along.

Stories about spiritual practitioners who enjoy spectacular results are legion. Somewhat less legion are stories about practitioners having the rug pulled out from under them. St. John of the Cross is the great chronicler of spiritual disappointment and frustration in the Christian tradition. St. John was immersed in communion with God, and then it all got ripped away from him. Slowly, over years, he had to make his way back. He coined the phrase "dark night of the soul" to describe this painful part of the journey. While beginners experience some disappointments, more advanced practitioners are kicked out of heaven for long periods of time, or so it feels to them. During the dark night, we find out about the depth of our attachments. We find out that we can be angry at God. We must revisit every karma, especially pride. We are dredged deeply and finally washed in God's compassion and love.[25]

You can sit down and do meditation or other practices for some years and feel pretty self-satisfied with your "great experiences." You can have certain accomplishments and become attached to them. You can brag about the high points, and you might even make big claims about your level of accomplishment. All you are proving is that you are stuck.

When somebody is *always* having a nice experience doing practice, or is telling a lot of stories about themselves, you can bet that attachment is happening. The only time a good teacher tells stories about their experiences is for the benefit of students. Students do need to hear about spiritual experiences, but when a teacher has a party piece they are repetitively shopping around, that is actually a sign of spiritual stagnation.

If you work with periods of discontent in a humble and sincere way, you discover a quality of openness that you really couldn't have imagined. Most often, discontent arises during periods when nothing seems to be happening in your practice. Yet a tremendous release of karma occurs if you submit to the energy of that discontent. If you learn not to antidote discontent with stories, or ego-driven effort, then you end up in a very different condition just when you thought nothing was happening.

Attachment to enjoyable spiritual experiences is a huge obstacle. It's difficult to get sober and deal with what's actually happening. It's like quitting heroin. Heroin is enjoyable up to a point, but it isn't really helping you to wake up. Longing must recognize its proper goals: to discover and rest in your real nature, to find permanent refuge in the eternal, to rediscover the enjoyment that needs no particular object or circumstances to sustain it. This is what we are longing for, but longing gets misplaced onto all of these other things. Sadhana recalibrates and redirects our longing so that we can discover real wisdom and lasting contentment.

Of course, we are not denouncing enjoyment in our sadhana. We should enjoy what is enjoyable, but also not hold onto it. We can follow a natural rhythm like waves coming to the shore and then receding again. We don't have to reject anything. We don't have to prove that we're spiritual by pushing away pleasures and satisfactions. That's silly. Wisdom is working with us. Wisdom is bringing us those satisfactions and wisdom is taking them away. So, what we want to do is have a light hand. We want to enjoy things, but then when it's time for them to go, let them go. This isn't easy advice to follow, and I certainly haven't always followed it myself.

Most of my life, since I was a little girl of three or four years old, I have had these spectacular, cosmic-sized dreams. I have received meaningful visions and teachings and initiations in dreams. I've gone to crazy, magical, beautiful places. I loved my dream life. I was so, so attached to it. And then, at some point, it all went away. I was incredibly pissed off about that, but I was just so attached to these kinds of dreams that they had to go until I let go. This is the action of grace.

You can experience feelings of contentment as a result of your practice, but as long as you are attached to certain experiences, you are going to experience discontentment at some point. All of our attachments have to go. The Guru principle—that which moves us toward awakening—helps us to discover that any attachment is a ball and chain. Discontentment is the force that eventually moves us to seek greater freedom.

FRUITS

FRUIT ONE
Delighting in expressing kindness

One time I was doing a particular sadhana for clearing six realm karmic vision. Every day I was doing this sadhana for many hours and sending out prayers for all beings to be released from suffering. Unexpectedly, other realm beings started coming to me for help. Some were animals. Some were hungry ghosts. They started showing up in dreams and visions. The teacher who gave me this practice hadn't mentioned this possibility! How to help suffering hungry ghosts wasn't in the instruction manual. I really had no idea what I was doing. But spontaneously I found myself making simple gestures of kindness.

One time a hungry ghost came and told me that it had done something terrible in a previous life and was suffering with overwhelming guilt. I didn't know what to do. So I just looked directly at this apparition and said, "It's okay. You did your best." In that moment, all of the tension and pain of this being visibly drained away. I saw its ghost form release and resolve back into the infinite with a sigh of deep relaxation and peace.

Many of us are completely wrapped up in self-concern. Other people appear only as gray shadows in the Theater of Me. As we wake up a bit, we begin to feel genuine kindness toward other people. We act in a way that we call selfless, but actually, we are acting in a Self-full way: full of awakened Self.

Sometimes people have the bizarre idea that, upon becoming more realized, they are going to be wandering around without any I-sense, or they are not going to have any experience of their bodies. They are going to be compassionate pink clouds or something. But "selfless" really means that you are experiencing your continuity with life. You are relating to the experience of others with the same degree of empathy with which you relate to yourself.

Kindness is the supreme medicine and the universal solvent. Kindness is the greatest siddhi. If you can experience genuine kindness toward all other beings, that is the accomplishment—not fancy yogic postures, magical powers, stopping your breath and thoughts, foreseeing the future, or taking a light body. Kindness is not a set of behaviors that you can download and start performing. Kindness is also not an attitude, or mental orientation. It is an abiding feeling, an abiding impulse, that springs from the natural desire for the welfare of others.

Kindness comes from an experience of deep empathy with other beings. You experience actual warmth toward others that expresses as a natural desire not to add to their karmic load, and in fact to lessen it. Kindness really emerges from experiencing the dazzling, Vajra nature of others, from an appreciation of the intrinsic value of others. Appreciation is so much more relevant than acceptance. Acceptance doesn't even make any sense. No one needs your acceptance. Everyone has a perfect, natural right to show up exactly as they are. Whether you do or do not accept someone, or something, is completely inconsequential. If you decide to be in a relationship with another person, you must appreciate them as they are. Otherwise, all of your relationships remain extremely superficial. It is not enough to just appreciate, in some intellectual way, a person's right to be how they are. You must actually enjoy how they are on some level, just as you would enjoy a work of art.

Our authentic appreciation of each other and our lives is on a continuum with the Supreme Being's enjoyment of the entirety of the creation. When you begin to experience that, you discover an unstoppable desire to help others to pull aside the karmic curtain and experience their own Vajra nature, joining you in that celebration and joy. Kindness helps people to wake up and discover who they really are, and ultimately kindness is motivated by the desire to see that happen.

Vajra Nature and Shiva Nature mean the same thing: the shared, essential ground of being which is indestructible, virtuous, and wise. When we begin to have the experience of the intrinsic value of ourselves and others, we begin to have more actual respect for other people.

Respect is a big word for me. My Dzogchen teacher, Namkhai Norbu Rinpoche, talks about having respect for another person's unique dimension. We all share Vajra or Shiva Nature, but each of us has a unique way of expressing that: a unique dimension. In other words, we are all like unique works of art. When we appreciate a work of art, we respect its integrity. We respect that it has shown up in a certain way, and that it is fine on its own terms. This is what is meant by respecting the other person's unique dimension. Even if you don't like something, or you don't want to be around something, you appreciate how the other person is, and you respect their right to show up exactly how they are showing up.

Intrinsic value has a much deeper significance than some sort of intellectual acceptance, or tolerance, or appreciating a person only when he or she is doing something you like. Intrinsic value means that you have the recognition that the other person's essence nature is the same as yours and that however they are showing up is an aspect or an expression of the indestructible essence nature of this reality, aka God. We all possess intrinsic value insofar as we are all expressions of and made of the same creative, alive, self-aware reality.

Of course, sometimes people ask, "What if I don't love myself? What if I am not kind to myself?" When we have feelings of self-hatred or of being lesser-than, we are in pain. We already know what happens when we're in pain. We're walking along, talking to our friends, and then we stub our toe. Suddenly our whole world becomes our toe. So when we're in pain, we lose the sense of continuity and connection with others. We can, in general, be quite self-concerned. So we have to develop a feeling of kindness toward ourselves before we can feel genuine kindness toward others. Long-term, consistent meditation practice can help us to develop a more friendly and kind feeling toward ourselves.

What I said about pain doesn't pertain if you are already somewhat established in the natural state. If you have enough of a base in the experience of continuity with others, you will not lose contact just because a pain happens. After practicing for a long time and realizing, you will no longer be distracted from your real condition, which is continuity. When you wake up more, all of the things that distract you when you are less awake no longer distract you. They are just things happening in a much bigger field of continuity. You don't get thrown off so easily. But when you're at the beginning, you do tend to get thrown off by any kind of pain or discomfort. This is a natural progression that unfolds as we practice day-by-day.

When you really begin to experience the intrinsic value of everything and everyone, of all the appearings of this world, then you naturally experience devotion. You can be delighted to *pranam* (bow) to a coffee cup, or an elephant, or a friend, or a tree, or anything. Everything is alive with that same intrinsic value, that same intelligence and artistry and wonder-provoking quality. At the root, you can experience a feeling of wonder that anything at all exists, rather than nothing. When your perceptions become more subtle and expansive, you begin to have a direct experience of how things are arising, from what they are arising, and what they are made of. Then devotion and kindness just pour out naturally toward everything.

I feel a sense of wonder and devotion toward everything that is appearing in this life. And I want all of you to be able to experience that too. I know that many of you have not discovered that, or maybe have only gotten glimpses of the intrinsic value of everyone and everything. I know that many of you are not yet in a condition in which you can feel the same overwhelming devotion for the lamp on your altar, for me, and for any other person. I have that experience every day as a result of my sadhana. I recognize that you also have that capacity. Whatever condition you're in, I recognize that you have, built into you, incontrovertible and indestructible, the capacity to have the same realization that I've had and more. I have the capacity to realize more, and so do you, because we have the same essence nature. We all have the same exact essence nature, and it inevitably leads us to experience caring and concern and appreciation for everything here.

Sometimes people have the experience that I am picky because I want things to be arranged in a certain way. I definitely *do* want things to be arranged in a certain way here in our teaching space so that people feel relaxed and comfortable and welcome. I want to do things in a certain way because I experience a caring feeling toward everyone who might be my guest or share a circumstance with me. This desire results from my practice and feeling, in a real way, that everyone I encounter is an aspect of God. I want you all, and anyone who might come in the future, to have the best possible opportunity to discover that. People can see the arrangements here in our teaching space, but they also consciously or subliminally understand that the community has cleaned and arranged the space, made tea, and set out cushions specifically for their comfort. Having the experience of being hosted well helps our guests to relax, and it also helps them to know God.

Even though there is a natural desire to support others to self-realize, the kindness and compassion expressed by a more awake person is not an earnest, heavy-handed situation. It isn't a do-gooder situation. When you actually relax karmic tensions and discover natural devotion, you delight in expressing kindness toward other beings. This delight is playful. You don't have the attitude that you are saving people or fixing people. You understand that your activities are how reality is playing its own game of waking up and recognizing itself. You are the musical instrument, not the master.

People ask, "How can I care more about other people? How can I be more compassionate?" In their voices is a fervent, urgent quality, and that's fine. That kind of overheated, earnest way of approaching care and concern for others manifests at the stage in which you still experience others as separate from you. They can be damaged and hurt and you have to do something to make them better. Or you feel averse to a person, and you urgently want to still show them compassion in spite of your feeling of recoil. That's where that earnestness comes from; it's just part of the journey, but it is not the destination.

At one time, I was very much in the same condition as most of you. I was miserable, defensive, aggressive, and overly self-concerned. I started doing sadhana when I was twenty-seven, and now I'm sixty-one. If you had told me at twenty-seven that I was going to end up feeling delight in expressing devotion to everyone and everything, I probably would have stopped going to teachings. The whole idea would have horrified me! "You mean feel devotion toward that jerk over there? No way!"

But slowly, over more than thirty years of daily practice, natural devotion arose. I found myself enjoying the unparalleled pleasure of expressing that devotion. Forget about concern for others being important—it is just divinely pleasurable to express! It is a delight that you can hardly imagine.

Imagine you, the student, are popcorn in a pan. The teachings and the lineage are the pot. The teacher and your sadhana are the fire. At first you are this hard kernel. You look really unappetizing, and one could hardly imagine that you'd end up tasty in any way.

Think how much fun this is for me, the teacher. "Oooh... I hear a pop! Oh, there's another one! Students are starting to smell really fragrant." There is delight in trying to do everything possible so that you all can have this experience and share it with me. This is what it's all about.

FRUIT TWO

Attending courageously and devotedly to the conditions that make it possible to realize

As we do spiritual practice over time, the desire to create and maintain the conditions that make it possible for us to realize naturally intensifies. One of the first fruits of our practice is the feeling that we don't want to miss opportunities to do sadhana and receive teachings. We can recognize these opportunities and respond to them in many different ways.

I started doing kundalini yoga and kriya yoga practices in my twenties, and things developed over a long period of time. When I first was starting to experience some openings, I would notice subtle energies moving in my body or entering my body in specific ways. It could happen at any time, not just when I was sitting on a meditation cushion. Whenever this happened, I would start doing sadhana. Even if I was driving, I would pull over to the side of the road and start doing some sadhana. Then, for many years, when I was about to go in a less than ideal direction, I would feel a pressure at the third eye between my eyebrows. It was as if my Guru had her thumb there and was saying, "Stop!" The desire to pay attention and follow and develop a relationship to these opportunities is the fruit of practice.

When some people have an opening, they just relate to that as a cool experience. They embalm it in spiritual bioplastic and display it pridefully. But spiritual experience is actually a gateway, a beginning, not a culmination. You are being shown that you have the capacity to develop a deeper level of sensitivity. It's not like God came and fiddled with you for a minute and showed you something that's not really an aspect of you. All spiritual experience is an aspect of you. You are being told to get to work and make it your new normal. You are being given an opportunity to grow, not a spiritual achievement badge.

Everybody can develop an "opportunity antenna." Everyone can learn to read and respond to the unique ways in which wisdom is speaking to them. Everyone can discover this through a process of deep listening and engagement. These wisdom signals can be read, and they can guide you.

I can give you another example. People find many ordinary mind reasons not to come to teachings, even when the heart wants to open to wisdom. I've seen this happen over and over again. I certainly have experienced this, too. I have stayed away from teachings because they were too far away, or too much money, or too much time. I've stayed away because I was tired, or I had promised somebody that I'd go to the movies with them. Our karmas fight to survive!

But when you feel that going to a particular teaching would be the right move for you, you can pause to notice that familiar inner feeling of goodness and sweetness. We should always try to follow when we have this type of heart-based response. This direct way of knowing and following is the primary method for meeting opportunities.

Most of us are trained to follow our ordinary, conceptual mind and the pull of reactive emotions. We may go so far as to obtain teachings, but we constantly declare "I can't do this and I can't do that" because of the demands of ordinary life, or fear. The fact is that we *can* organize our lives around waking up. We just need to listen to the promptings of the wisdom emanating from our own hearts. That wisdom is always victorious.

If your desire to wake up is strong, you will try hard not to miss opportunity. You will make heroic efforts. You will do it out of your own desire. The more your senses open up, the more you will sense opportunity and have the desire to follow it. Natural law dictates that the more you take opportunity, the more opportunity will come your way. You will progress like this.

The desire to wake up can become quite ferocious. You aren't going to let anything stand in your way! Work is not going to stand in your way. Relationships are not going to stand in your way. Poverty is not going to stand in your way. Having to travel long distances, or to move, is not going to stand in your way. No fear or dogmatic concept is going to stand in your way. In some instances, not even illness is going to stand in your way. If you already feel like this, you probably have done a lot of practice in this life or previous lives. Experiencing the unstoppable desire to wake up and discover your real nature is one of the supreme fruits of having done a lot of practice.

At some point, you also begin to naturally desire to support the conditions that help *other* people to realize. You definitely don't want to hinder another person from practicing, or getting teachings. In fact, you come to recognize that as the most difficult form of karmic entanglement. On the other hand, sometimes people develop an ego attachment to the idea that they are doing spiritual practice only to help *other* people. But the best possible way to be of service to others is to have some realization yourself. You have to pay attention to the conditions that help you to realize before you can develop a real understanding of what conditions make it possible for other people to realize. That wisdom can only be gotten firsthand by practicing.

Often people practice for a long time before their desire to wake up supersedes their desire to keep on doing what they have always done. The main culprit is karmic momentum. Karma means temporary patterns of consciousness and energy that repeat in time. Karmas have real momentum; they have force. The momentum of karma manifests as desire. We desire to do something, or to not do something, or to remain in a situation or to not remain in a situation. The fervent desire to receive teachings and do sadhana is also the result of conditioning. But this kind of conditioning ultimately leads one to the unconditioned.

Many years ago when I lived in Berkeley, Shambhala was hosting a teaching with a certain visiting Rinpoche. I had long wanted to take teachings from this Rinpoche. At the same time as the teaching, a friend was throwing herself a fortieth birthday party. I had a dilemma. Should I go to the teaching, or should I go to my friend's birthday party? I arrived at what I thought was a good solution. I went to the party for fifteen minutes, which then allowed me to get to the teaching on time. It turned out to be one of the most important teachings I have ever received. But my friend was still angry with me. The friendship did not survive.

I had already been practicing for many years when this circumstance arose. The desire to wake up was relatively strong. But at certain points in our unfolding, the answer would clearly be that we should go to the birthday party. We love our friend, and we don't want our friend to feel upset. We also anticipate having a lot of fun at the party, and we simply wouldn't miss it for the world! There is no contest. Yet at another point, we might feel more ambivalent. And at yet another point, if we feel it may help to create the conditions for greater realization, we will go to the teaching.

We need courage to make the adjustments in our lives that allow us to receive teachings, do sadhana, and align with wisdom. We may end up adjusting or changing our job, our relationships, and our habits of eating and sleeping. It takes courage and clarity, and most of all desire, to change those things. Some people strongly resist change. They feel a sincere longing for a new circumstance, but the barriers to creating change, even to get what they actually want, seem insurmountable. Other people resist change by compartmentalizing their lives. They will set up a little altar in the corner of a bedroom and do some practice each morning, but the bedroom door is where they draw the line between spiritual life and everything else.

Whatever anyone is doing, they are acting according to their desire based on the momentum of karma. So there is no blame or shame. These karmas are totally natural and are expressions of the creativity of God. But there does come a point when you have seen who you really are, when you have seen how things actually are, that the desire to realize grows. This is when you become what is called a "non-returner." That's kind of a silly term because actually, we're all non-returners. True, we are all coming and going, in and out of states of greater awareness and greater ignorance. We go back and forth, vacillating between different degrees of awareness. But we are all on the same trajectory. It's not a straight line, but we are all moving in the same general direction toward awakening. How do I know this? Because every sentient being longs for sweetness, for connection, and ultimately for self-knowledge, even though most often this longing expresses itself in a limited way. That longing is the voice of God, of Guru, of our own Self urging us on.

When you become a non-returner, it means that the desire to realize has grown strong enough to overwhelm a lot of the karmic momentum that has been driving you. The experience of trudging along doing your sadhana in an individualistic way begins to give way to a more effortless experience. You realize that you're in a conversation: wisdom is speaking to you. You also learn how to open and respond. Increasingly, you have the direct understanding that you are being guided. You finally recognize that your job is not to push and trudge and struggle, but to listen and follow. Sadhana becomes more like the effort of going to meet a lover than the effort of slogging through mud on a lonely pathway.

Ultimately, engaging in the process of waking up, whatever that entails, becomes a choiceless choice. This happened to me immediately. I was a non-returner from the moment I met this tradition. Something in me just said yes, and I never looked back. I have learned through working with students that my experience is somewhat unusual, but everyone gets to that point eventually. No matter how much you struggle, or try to use your ordinary mind to fight against it, or throw doubts at it, you just aren't walking away. You're done. This is called a choiceless choice. You made a choice, but it wasn't a choice that you could *not* have made.

When you are conscious of the fact that the choice has been made, a very deep relaxation takes place. This condition is also described as being in the river. You are no longer treading water in the shallows, or standing by on the banks. You are in the middle of the river, and a strong current is carrying you. You are immersed in the waters of devotion. Devotion naturally manifests as the desire that other people be relieved of suffering. You now recognize the supreme nourishment and the real meaning of refuge. You know that the wisdom of Self-knowledge resolves all karma. You just want everybody to have that opportunity and that experience. So, slowly, over time, you become more devoted to creating conditions for other people to realize.

The degree to which you torture other people with your own fixations starts to diminish. You no longer desire to perpetuate other people's suffering. You begin to consciously look for opportunities to help other people relax. You also lose any desire to criticize other traditions. You stop comparing or claiming that your tradition is the best or the greatest or the highest. You see that all of the streams of teachings are aspects of one process, ongoing everywhere.

Fruit Two

FRUIT THREE
Delighting in the play of alliance

I do divination with an older form of the Yi Jing called the Zhouyi. One of the central values of the text is alliance. The Zhouyi teaches us that we cannot mine the potential we bring into this life unless we skillfully and willingly enter into alliances with other beings and circumstances.[26]

We each arrive here with different capacities. We also arrive with deficits of capacity, areas of our functioning in which our minds are clouded by confusion, or our senses are dulled, or our bodies are inept. Maybe we are skilled at doing intellectual work such as analysis or mathematics or writing research papers. But then when it comes to money, we're just a disaster. We may be clear-sighted in some areas of our lives, but have a hard time navigating other areas. All of this has to do with the particular packages of karmas that we carry. Alliance helps us to reach our potential in areas where we have natural capacity and to get support in areas where we aren't so well-endowed.

One of the symptoms of waking up a little bit more is that you begin to feel grateful that you have help. You begin to notice how you are being helped in many different circumstances in both obvious and subtle ways. You begin to feel, "Whew, I'm glad I'm not out here on my own. I'm glad that someone or wisdom itself is paying attention and is creating opportunities for me to be in alliance with other people." The sense of shame no longer arises when you need to ask for help. You no longer feel any kind of reluctance or holding back or defensiveness when you meet people who can help you, including spiritual teachers. You are no longer defending that sense of independent individuality. You realize how inadequate that construct is—and that it is just a construct.

We couldn't really ever name or know all of the alliances in which we participate. We are in alliances with our friends and our family and our spiritual communities and our co-workers. We're in alliance with our ancestors. We're in national and cultural alliances. We're in alliance with teachers who are not present in this life. We're in alliance with many other beings who feed us and make our world habitable and beautiful. We are in alliance with rivers and trees and bees and oceans and space. The diversity of alliance allows for the creation of diverse, creative expressions.

The pulse between union and diversity is fundamental to reality. In Trika Shaivism, we personify all of reality as Shiva and Shakti, a male and female aspect who are eternally united, but who have the power to create experiences of diversity. Furthermore, all of manifest reality is described as being composed of unified zones of creative potential, or *andas*. Anda means egg. Within these fertile zones, experiences of diversity arise. Out of the one arises the display of the many. That's what we're playing with when we play with alliances. When we dance in and out of different alliances to create diverse experiences and forms of life, we are enacting the pulse of creation.

When we are more realized, we have direct perceptions of the natural state of continuity. We still experience the play of diversity, but only as the arising of an appearance of separation. I still see you sitting over there, but at the same time, I don't have a definite experience of us being separate anymore. I feel our continuity in a tangible, incontrovertible way. So being in touch with the continuity of living presence does not mean that you don't have an experience of the play of diversity. It just means that you don't actually feel separate. It means that you don't defend your separateness, or insist on it, or have a "go it alone" attitude. Suffering subsides, and you can enjoy the display.

When we are more awake, we understand that nothing happens without alliance. We know that we have to participate wholeheartedly in alliances if we want to have a fruitful life. We actually can delight in that play of alliance. We can enjoy how alliances form and change and create new possibilities for self-expression and creativity. We begin to recognize nourishment in all of those circumstances. We begin to feel happy and grateful that those situations even exist. We begin to participate with a sense of joy and curiosity and gusto. Going along with interdependency is not a utilitarian gesture; it is actually a source of deep delight.

FRUIT FOUR

Participating in the play of continuous conversation

When we are immersed in the base state of alive awareness, we are in a total communicative situation. Manifest life is a theater in which unconditioned awareness shows up in diverse forms and contemplates its own nature through infinite, interactive circumstances and a continuous flow of conversation.

Communication, or conversation, is a large part of the fun of this world. In the Shakta Tantrik tradition of West Bengal, all of manifest life is compared to a great metropolis full of entertainments and commerce.[27] We visit cities in order to experience diversity, communication with others, and less limited forms of self-expression. Until our senses are more open, we only have the capacity to participate in a very small number of the conversations. We live in the city, but we are holed up in our tiny apartments much of the time. Our bandwidth is really limited! The Tantrik siddha does not seek to withdraw, but rather to leave limitation behind and become immersed in the city of manifest life as a *jivanmukta*, one who is liberated in life.

Humans embody a wide range of sensitivities, or lack of sensitivity to the world conversation. When I was in graduate school, a young professor told me that he could not sense how other people were feeling. Other people are more observant and empathic. Most of us participate in ordinary kinds of conversations with human beings. Many people feel able to communicate with animals. Other people notice the communication of their bodies, energy, and mind with the changing weather and seasons. In fact, every cell in our bodies is communicating with our environment, both external and internal.

When you become more sensitive, you start to notice the pervasive subtle conversations in which you have always been immersed. You can notice the subtle moods of others. You can notice subtle, communicative movements of energy. You can communicate with your ancestors. You can receive transmission from your teacher, or even teachers in dreams and visions. You can naturally understand the language of ritual. You can notice and read omens and more specialized kinds of communications. You can directly sense when the proper time has arrived for some particular activity. Most importantly, you can participate more consciously. You can sense the wisdom that is prompting you at every turn, whether it speaks from the mouth of nature, a teacher, another person, a circumstance, or your own wisdom heart.

When I first began to feel the vastness of cause and effect that operates in our relative experience, I found it quite intimidating. I could sense more of the communication happening all around me, but I was still speaking baby language. All around me, and inside myself, I began to notice the guiding hand of Guru. I felt so inept! It is easier to follow the advice of an external, human Guru who speaks to you in a conventional way. But when all circumstances are Guru, and you want to decipher that, it can be a little overwhelming. At the same time, it is wondrous when we begin to notice the subtler types of communication.

As we experience more of our continuity with infinite, alive awareness, our senses begin to lose their boundaries. You can compare this to a tributary or a creek making its way back to a mighty river and eventually, to the ocean. The senses of this alive aware reality, aka God, are infinite. In fact, our limited senses *are* the senses of God, stepped down. Hearing, seeing, smelling, touching, tasting, and sensing with the mind are all capacities of this alive, aware reality. We don't really "have" senses; we participate in *the* senses of the entire reality. The relaxation and refinement of our senses that takes place due to sadhana is actually an outcome of the erosion of our feeling of separation.

Many of us forget to reach out and meet life directly with our senses. In fact, we mistrust our direct experience due to our culture's over-valuing of thinking. The result is that we often feel quite separate and locked up inside of ordinary mind. We lose the capacity to surrender our boundaries and become immersed in the conversation of our senses with manifest life. We experience livingness and its play of conversation through a filter of concepts and thoughts. This creates a situation in which our ordinary senses tend to become deadened. Sadhana can feel dry and boring when you are relating to it only through your ordinary, conceptual mind.

The core method of direct realization practice is to integrate your awareness and energy with unconditioned presence. Being able to directly sense the intelligence and energy in which you are already immersed is the first step toward participating in the play of continuous conversation. Primordial intelligence involves much more than just how well we string thoughts together, how logical we are, or how quick we are. Primordial intelligence is the inherent, omnipresent capacity of reality to directly know its own nature.

The function of primordial intelligence, as it shows up in us, is to reach into a circumstance or into an experiential field and find out about it through an open-ended, curious, exploratory, experimental process. Every cell in your body has intelligence. You can see

Fruit Four

this most clearly when you contemplate your other senses: hearing, vision, touch, smell, and taste. When you engage these senses, you are reaching out or into an aspect of reality to discover it, to meet it. All of the senses, including mind, have this aspect of curiosity about how things are.

Primordial intelligence is never done exploring. It has no goal other than enjoyment. Unlike ordinary intellect, it doesn't want to complete something or wrap something up or come to a final conclusion. Primordial intelligence operates more as a dialogue or a conversation. It is in dialogue with sense experiences and the objects of the senses and ultimately with its own creations.

A special class of instruction given to students in direct realization traditions is called "pointing out instructions." These are instructions for doing things in your sadhana that no one can actually tell you how to do. The teacher can only point toward the goal, but cannot precisely tell you how to reach it. You have to make a leap into direct experience. These are considered to be the most important instructions a student receives from a teacher.

Some students find it extremely difficult to grasp the nature of pointing out instructions. It's like a disconnect has occurred, and they have to rebuild the bridges to their senses and direct experience. They are trying to communicate with life using only tin cans connected by a string. They have to remember the difference between thinking about something and experiencing it in a more full, sensory, immersive way.

Transmission is a word that direct realization traditions use to describe an experience of entering into a more immersive experience of essence nature with the help of a teacher. Of course, there is nothing but essence nature. It is always "transmitting." We are always immersed. But as students with limitations, we often need a special circumstance to help us to notice and experience that. It is the job of the teacher to orchestrate such circumstances and try to help students to recognize their real nature. Transmission is not an intellectual or conceptual affair. Transmission communicates to you by revealing something about your real nature to you in a direct, experiential way.

There are two related Sanskrit phrases that help us to understand transmission. One is *pratyaksha darshana* and the other is *pratyaksha pramana*. Pratyaksha darshana means to see directly, where "seeing" means recognizing, not just ordinary seeing. Pratyaksha pramana means to explore something for yourself or to experiment or find out for yourself. It's the "noodling around" factor. Transmission is not just about being passive and getting something from the teacher. It's about working with the transmission and discovering *that* in yourself. Transmission reconnects you to what you already are, but you have to work to explore and stabilize that recognition. The whole point is to give you a taste of primordial continuity and wisdom so that you can find your way back to that on your own. Transmission is a beacon, or an open door. You have to follow and walk through the door.

Often teachers make a big deal about transmission. I have witnessed teachers dangling transmission in front of students as a prize to chase after. Sometimes teachers charge large amounts of money for *shaktipat*, or formal transmission, and promise salvation to people who ante up. This is ridiculous. When a teacher gives transmission, they are acting as an appliance to amplify what is already pervasive and generously available to all beings. We need the appliance only until we can hear and feel on our own. We may benefit when the teacher stages a set of formal circumstances, such as a ritual or initiation. But this is just to focus attention and create a greater possibility for students to notice and tune into what is in fact happening all the time everywhere.

Via word, sight, or touch, or even more subtle means, transmission is how you can have a direct experience of enlightened essence nature even in the early stages of your life as a practitioner. You are not receiving something outside of yourself during transmission.

The teacher is not giving you something you don't already possess. You are not a beggar at the door. However fully you are able to enter into it, transmission is the experience of being able to sense the intelligence and energy directing the conversation in which you are already immersed.

FRUIT FIVE

Delighting in skillfully adapting to the play of circumstance

Life never turns out exactly as planned, and it inevitably includes a healthy share of loss and discomfort. You simply *are* going to have to adapt to unpredictable, natural ups and downs. When we come to a circumstance with a lot of concepts about what success means, there is just no way that we can adapt skillfully. We cannot feel, see, or relate to the situation as it actually is.

Success is often *not* about reaching a goal or achieving an outcome that we set out to achieve. This is so obvious, but we forget about it all the time. Think of when you were younger and were attached to a lover. Maybe in some moment you thought that you wanted to be with that person forever. Then after some time goes by, you break up. It's devastating. You think you will never recover. Then more time goes by. Now you think the opposite. You are so grateful not to be with that person. You now see the breakup as a great boon. The idea that you might have actually ended up with what you once wanted so fervently is somewhat horrifying.

You might have the attitude that there is something existentially wrong with a particular outcome. That is *never* true. Nothing has ever gone wrong. You are just having a human life. If you waste your time thinking about what has "gone wrong" and how you want it to be a different way, then you are one step, or two, or three, or four, or five steps removed from present circumstance. You are removed from the immediacy of what's happening and then you cannot relate to life skillfully. Even if you found yourself in a prison camp in Siberia, it would not be wrong in that existential sense. It would simply be the circumstance that you've been given to work with. And your job would be the same, on one level, as working with the circumstance of deciding whether you should eat a gelato after reading this book.

Life inevitably does not play by your rules or according to your expectations. As Tantrikas, we are just being in presence with our minds and our senses open. We don't over plan or pre-define how success looks. We're not telling ourselves, "I can be successful in every circumstance." We're telling ourselves, "I can work with every circumstance. I can skillfully adapt. I can communicate with every circumstance." And then, whatever happens, happens.

When you are more relaxed, aka more awake, the play of circumstance is actually enjoyable. Whether painful or wonderful, the extraordinary variety of circumstances is engaging, rich, astounding, and often funny. The fact that you get handed a hard problem is on some level fun. You can experience the beauty in feeling sad and crying. Destruction and loss share a somewhat thrilling quality. Even physical pain is interesting. When outcomes surprise you, whether in a happy or painful way, there is joy in the dance-like capacity to adapt smoothly and skillfully. All in all, I would say that life becomes more like an amusement park ride, or a dance festival, or like surfing, and less like a daytime soap opera.

Even imprisonment is not 100 percent horrible if you're being a practitioner. If you're being an ordinary person, it's terrible, absolutely terrible. Yet you can read the memoirs of Lamas and Rinpoches who escaped or were released from Chinese prison camps. Their life was excruciatingly hard. They were tortured, worked nearly to death, isolated, cold, and starving. At the same time, some who approached their circumstance thoroughly as sadhana don't regret having been imprisoned.[28]

This alive, aware reality gives us circumstances to work with that are appropriate for us. Sometimes our trials and tribulations are really not all that difficult. But then we have the limit cases. We can be pushed to the limit of our capacity. If we can recognize the opportunity in this, we can experience real grace and transformation in our lives.

When we have practiced well and are receiving wisdom's myriad communications, then we can recognize the loving intent of this reality in everything that happens here. We don't have to make anything up, or chant aphorisms, or embellish. Compassion, intelligence, and mercy are actually present and tangible in full measure in every situation. Most of us know that when difficult situations happen, wisdom is present. But a lot of us, even having recognized that, walk away cursing. We just don't want our habitual patterns to be challenged or disrupted. We don't yet feel the grace in that. We don't yet feel the compassion in that.

When you are more realized, you will feel delight in communicating skillfully, adapting skillfully, and relating to the wisdom in every situation. The Board of Directors of Jaya Kula has been talking about this. When we were only on the West Coast, we grew quickly. Many people on the West Coast are interested in Indian and Tibetan spirituality. Some people even know about Trika Shaivism. The core community grew steadily. This pattern continued until I moved to Maine.

Because of our steady growth, our method of budgeting assumed that Jaya Kula would enjoy an increase in income every year. But since we moved to Maine, the situation has changed. Because of the View, the Board understands that we have to adapt. We can't plan

157

Fruit Five

based on the hope that things have slowed down only in a temporary way. We don't know what will happen. We can only try to work with the immediacy of our circumstance. We are situated in a part of the country with a different culture. We can't force it to be like the West Coast. We have to change how we plan financially. At one point, I said to our Board treasurer, "This is kind of fun! It's kind of sexy having to tighten our belts!" A new circumstance has arisen. The budgeting process has suddenly gotten more interesting.

This is just a little example of how you work with changing circumstances. You don't proclaim, "We have to get more people! We have to grow! We have to keep it all going!" I'm certainly not going to hit the streets with a sandwich board to try to magnetize more people! We just try to adapt as gracefully as we are able. It's fun to do that. Adaptation can have a game app quality. If we're not attached to things turning out in a particular way, we can have this experience.

I've always noticed how six-month old babies sit in a beautiful way with absolutely perfect posture. They have no rigidity. Despite their upright posture, they are free to move spontaneously in any direction at any moment. Their eyes, faces, and entire bodies are poised in the attitude of delighted expectancy. "What can I relate to next? What can I discover next?" This is how we want to practice, and this is how we want to live: poised and porous and responding with freshness and spontaneity to what is actually happening, not to our idea of what should happen.

As we go along, we also learn about the value of waiting and still-ness. Anandamayi Ma said, "Relying entirely upon Him, keep still and watch what happens."[29] What a beautiful practice. When you are in some circumstance, some social circumstance, or in a classroom, or at work, you can practice standing still. Standing still doesn't mean not doing anything. It means don't perform anything. Don't push anything out. Don't plan anything. Don't promote anything. Don't try to make anything happen. Don't put out any undue effort, and just see what happens. Practice a kind of dynamic neutrality. There is a feeling of softness and openness. You're just waiting to see what happens. Something inevitably does happen, and then you can respond in an improvisational, spontaneous way. It's a beautiful sadhana to try.

FRUIT SIX

Tasting the sweetness of everything

Rasa means "taste" in Sanskrit. But in the spiritual traditions of India, and particularly in Trika Shaivism, it has a somewhat more profound array of meanings. It signifies the essential taste of existence. For this reason, rasa implies sweetness. When we are not suffering from limitation, the essential taste of existence itself is sweet. Rasa is also related to aesthetic enjoyment. In English, we say someone has "good taste" to indicate their aesthetic sophistication. The ananda of God is something like a profound aesthetic enjoyment of all of reality.

Sweet taste comes in many different forms. According to the Chinese and Ayurvedic traditions, most of the food that we eat is sweet. All grains have a fundamentally sweet taste. Meats have a sweet taste. These foods contain other tastes, too, but their predominant taste is sweet. Of course, anything with sugar in it is sweet. So if you reflect on your diet, you will probably recognize that you're mainly eating sweet taste. In the U.S., sweet, salty, and maybe a smattering of pungent and sour dominate our meals. We often leave

SHAMBHAVI SARASVATI

out bitter and astringent. We have to consciously add these back into our diet.

We have the understanding in this tradition that there is only one sweetness, and it expresses itself in many different ways. Everything here is a more or less limited reflection of the nature of the supreme reality. The sweet taste that we get at Dunkin Donuts is an extremely limited reflection of the sweet taste of existence itself. We also crave sweet relationships and sweet moments. In craving sweetness in all aspects of our lives, we are ultimately expressing our craving to be immersed in the divine.

When we do consistent spiritual practice, we eventually notice the limitations of ordinary sweet tastes, and our craving for these subsides. We can enjoy chocolate, but we don't hanker after it because we know that ordinary sweetness cannot satisfy our primordial longing. We can enjoy special friendships, but instead of feeling that a particular relationship is going to resolve our longing, we know that only discovering our real nature will do that.

Maybe at first we just switch from Dunkin Donuts to Holy Donuts. That's a fancier, healthier donut shop in Portland, Maine! I told you the story about eating yogurt for the first time as a kid. That yogurt was a weird substance! It looked and tasted like something that was mixed with chemicals and extruded from a machine. It really didn't smell or taste like anything living. But it had a lot of sugar in it, so I enjoyed it until my taste refined.

There is nothing wrong on an absolute level with those rather compromised pleasures we used to enjoy. It's just that they are, on a relative level, expressions of ignorance, or of limitation. Stuffing a cow full of antibiotics and hormones; imprisoning it; pumping milk out of it with a machine; treating the milk so that everything alive in it dies; processing the milk; stuffing it with more chemicals, processed sugar, and processed preserves; adding stabilizers, guar gum, food coloring, and other stuff to create that weird shiny consistency; and finally calling it "yogurt," is a product of ignorance. Greed is a form of ignorance, and compulsive greed is the main ingredient of bad food. We no longer want to eat that. We want to taste wisdom; we want to taste freedom from compulsion.

Rasa is outside of any relative consideration of good as opposed to bad. The primordial goodness, or sweetness, of existence stands on its own with no opposite. Perhaps you can feel that sweetness and the heart of wisdom within yourself as that which offers unfailing guidance and refuge. If you really want to be straight with yourself, if you really want to be on track with nature and other people, you can follow this immanent goodness. It supersedes everything. Our essential sweetness is called adamantine and unbreakable—like diamonds. When you're more relaxed and awake, and you have made contact with the beneficent wisdom that pours out of every crevasse of reality, then you can taste that unbreakable goodness continually. You can really feel that and align yourself with that continually. It is the Compass and the Friend.

Whatever your condition, right now you can point yourself in the direction of discovering primordial sweetness using just your ordinary mind. Think about your core values, your bottom lines. You can feel for your own integrity and stick to that. You can make a home there. But you must stick to your integrity no matter what happens. That's the way to find your ground in an ordinary sense. If you stand on your own integrity and refuse to budge, you will eventually begin to taste more of that primordial rasa.

Our relative core values, or ordinary sense of what is right and good, can set us in the direction of unconditioned goodness. This is why we have precepts in spiritual traditions. We try to express our shared core values and stick to them. This is functional, not moralistic. How would you need to show up right now in every part of your life in order to maintain your integrity in a pristine, uncompromised way? This is the question you want to ask yourself.

I confronted this question when I was in my twenties. I worked in conflicted situations with and for groups of people who were really poor, and at times very angry. One job was doing tenant organizing; the other was raising money for farmworker legal services. Sometimes I would get called "kike" or "dyke." Also, I was privileged in various ways in comparison to some of the people with whom I worked. In order to remain effective in my job, I decided that I would never lie or even exaggerate, that I would never promise to do more than I could deliver, and that I would always deliver what I promised. I just stood firm on that rock and let the storms swirl around me. And it was great. I learned so much. I learned that my integrity did not depend on being liked or approved of. It didn't depend on people treating me in a certain way. It didn't depend on people's opinions about me. I also learned that I could be a trustworthy ally and do my job thoroughly no matter what, and here I mean ally to both myself and others.

A lot of people are looking for validation rather than value. Looking for external validation rather than looking for existential value is a huge mistake. You get into worlds of emotional trouble and other kinds of trouble, too. There is no lasting value in external validation. You are looking to impermanence for the solution to the anxiety you feel about your existence. One person loves what you just did, another person hates it. One person thinks you're an angel, another person thinks you're a bitch. I mean there's just no ground. One minute you're happy with how people think of you, and the next minute you're devastated. You have one success, and you're thrilled; you have a failure, and you're in bed and on drugs for a week. But if you take refuge in your own integrity, even if you fail at something, it doesn't threaten you in any significant way because you are standing on the ground of real value.

If we are going to talk about following our sense of primordial sweetness, we must also talk about clarity. Primordial sweetness is not some ordinary, gooey feeling of going along with comforting karmic patterns. It blazes with supreme clarity. This requires courage to see, and it demands a warrior quality from anyone who

Fruit Six

follows it. It doesn't tell you to go in the direction that is well-worn. It tells you to go in the direction of waking up at all times without compromise. It is essentially indescribable, but it is *not* unknowable. You know it with all of your senses and your real intelligence. And it asks you to recalibrate to its all-encompassing, blazingly alive quality.

For example, people talk about compassion. What they are usually talking about is a terribly pale, anemic echo of that natural wisdom virtue. Speaking of "cultivating compassion," is like claiming you are going to cultivate an earthquake, or volcano, or even something like the birth of a star. My Guru, Anandamayi Ma, showed me the real nature of compassion. It poured out from everywhere like a mighty, roaring river. It brought me to my knees. I have spent the rest of my life since that revelation trying to open and embody that natural compassion and primordial intelligence directly. It's not something that you can cultivate; you can only attempt to open and allow it to possess you.

In this practice, learning and embodying are the same thing. We are never talking about just intellectual learning. When you are learning, you are feeling. You are getting accustomed to new feeling-perceptions with your senses and your mind. Some things that we learn about reality are hard to digest, and we avoid them or put them off for a time. Today I had a moment of intense, direct insight. When I say insight, I don't mean my mind thought something. I mean "being in the sight of." At the time, I didn't really want to go into it too much because I had a lot of work to do! That's how it is sometimes. We sense that opening to a greater reality is going to mess up our organized little world. We just want to attend to something more ordinary and limited, or we fear we are going to end up unprepared in new territory.

Anandamayi Ma's key teaching is that knowing yourself is equal to knowing God. That knowing is all-encompassing. You know it with every part of you. Sometimes we hold onto more familiar forms of sweetness for too long because we are afraid of that bigger sweetness. We are actually avoiding waking up. There have been times when I deliberately slowed down my practice because I just couldn't absorb what was happening. I couldn't stay with it. I had to back off for a time. I think this happens to everyone at some point.

Grace continually spills out from the heart of reality. Lord Shiva overflows excitedly with the impulse to create, to express the infinity of what can be expressed, to express his own infinite potential. When we begin to open our senses more and relax our self-concept, we have a more naked, immediate experience of the blazing, alive quality of reality. Many other teachers have described the process of sadhana as a process of acclimatization or of becoming accustomed to a more open condition. A good deal of adventurousness and willingness to step off into the unknown is required to do this practice. But even if we are adventurous, we still back off at times. Nobody keeps going full-on the whole time.

When we are distracted from wisdom, we take detours. We follow our pleasures, ambitions, and fears until we circle back and encounter a moment when we can hear wisdom again. We get another chance! Eventually we realize that even the detour is wisdom; it's just the long way around. Sometimes our karmic patterns are very strong, and they limit our ability to follow. But this is what sadhana is for, and eventually we find a way to follow wisdom the first time, every time.

Fruit Six

FRUIT SEVEN

Recognizing the equality of all phenomena

Anandamayi Ma described two hallmarks of self-realization. One is that you are able to experience what lies beyond the experience of linear time, giving rise to the experience of linear time. She called this the Supreme Moment.[30] Then she said that you realize the equality of all phenomena.[31] All of the great direct realization teachers from both Indian and Tibetan traditions have taught the same.

But before we get to equality, first let's talk about the *in*equality of all phenomena. We are already all too familiar with the inequality of all phenomena. We hold concepts and then create all kinds of judgments in our day-to-day lives about what is good or bad and right or wrong. We decide who is worthy or unworthy. We decide who to love, who to just like, and who to dislike or even hate. Operating with ordinary karmic mind, we pretty much divide everything and everyone up according to these sorts of "discernments."

Not only do we divide to conquer, but we are often convinced that our concepts, our opinions, and our judgments are absolute in their faithfulness to reality. If you say, "I don't like green beans," you can recognize this as a karmic situation that is not very important and maybe even funny. But if you claim, "Green beans suck," you are stuck with mistaking karmic vision for an absolute. Instead of practicing sane self-irony, you claim that's the way things are in some fundamental way. Of course, karmic visions are faithful to *your* reality—the reality inside your head. Or perhaps they are functional with respect to your relative experience (you don't like green beans because they make you sick). But that is the most you can say.

Gossip around the spiritual water cooler has it that realized people are not supposed to have preferences. This is generally understood in a rather unsubtle way. People think that having no preferences means that you don't make choices about what circumstances and people to engage with. But even if we are able to host and digest a wide range of people and circumstances, we are still using our discernment. Discernment and preferences are not the same thing.

People with intelligence and any degree of awakeness will make functional choices based on discerning what is dharmic, or supporting of waking up, and what is adharmic. They try to engage in relationships and circumstances that allow them to use their energy according to their innate sense of value. You may choose to have dinner with one set of people because you feel enlivened and enriched and nourished after spending time with them. You may decide not to dine with another set of people because you feel drained afterward. Maybe you are going to eat one thing over another because of your health. A more realized person will use natural discernment to support their practice, the teachings, and the well-being of people in general.

It is unskillful to try to pretend that you have no preferences. When I was much younger, and much less skillful, I briefly shared an apartment with a fellow practitioner. During that time, I was doing seated practice for sometimes six or seven hours a day. My roommate and I had discussed our lifestyles before moving in together.

It turned out that she sincerely *wanted* to do a lot of sadhana, but in reality, she couldn't sustain much. As I remember, she did sustain watching quite a bit of daytime TV! At the time, I couldn't stand hearing the sound of a TV for even short periods. We got into an intense situation around these differences and others. But we both had the idea that, as Tantrikas, we should be able to host any situation. So we kept slogging on through, becoming increasingly miserable. At one point, I went to see my acupuncturist. He was alarmed at the state of my health and urged me to get my own apartment. Eventually I dropped my concepts about the condition I thought, as a good Tantrika, I should be in. I moved into a different apartment. My health improved nearly instantaneously.

The point is that recognizing the equality of all phenomena doesn't have anything to do with surrendering our discernment, or functional preferences. We are also not saying that everything is the same. Everything is quite the opposite of "the same." Our reality is made up of infinite and wildly diverse manifestations. On the relative level, Chubby Hubby ice cream is not the same as Cherry Garcia ice cream. And using my partially enlightened discrimination, I can state with confidence that Cherry Garcia is slightly better for me, functionally speaking of course.

So what is it that we recognize when we realize the equality of all phenomena? We have the understanding in Trika Shaivism, but also in the other direct realization traditions such as Dzogchen, that there is a base reality from which all phenomena are arising. All phenomena, no matter how they appear from a relative perspective, are made of and by wisdom and its energy. You could visualize this as a great shining ocean with waves arising and subsiding. The reason we use the image of the ocean is because it appears naturally during meditation. It is not arbitrary; it is a living symbol that can teach us about reality.

I remember the first time I ever experienced this while I was meditating. I saw a great, shining, silvery ocean. My thoughts were

Fruit Seven

like raindrops rising from the ocean and falling back into the waters. It was very, very beautiful and peaceful. Through this living symbol, I saw the real nature of our thoughts, that they are all made of the ocean of consciousness and that they arise and subside naturally from the unconditioned. I never related to thoughts as enemies after this. I realized that thoughts are essence nature. I realized that all thoughts have total equality on this level. Whether I am thinking one kind of thought or another, there is nothing to get upset about.

The recognition of the equality of all phenomena is not like saying everything is made of atoms. At this point, most scientists cognize atoms as matter and energy, but not as consciousness or wisdom. My direct experience is that the unconditioned base state is literally made of, or full of, wisdom virtues such as intelligence, creativity, clarity, compassion, mercy, and curiosity, unending curiosity. So when we experience phenomena as being made of, made by, or arising from consciousness and energy, we're not just talking on the level of physics.

Recognizing that all circumstances are full of wisdom and made of wisdom, or God, is truly what is meant by realizing the equality of all phenomena. We can directly experience everything, including ourselves, as being goodness without an opposite. We can see for ourselves that objects, beings, and worlds are appearings of the light of consciousness: wise, playful, creative, compassionate, and kind. The appearings of the supreme reality have no independent existence, just as a wave cannot swim away from the ocean because it *is* ocean. This is the absolute View. Because of this, we can also understand that all phenomena are equal and always *perfect and fine*.

Of course, you may have all kinds of objections based on your perception of the vast field of birth, death, and suffering we call *samsara*. But the direct realization traditions teach that attachment to *nirvana,* or opposing nirvana to samsara, is also suffering. Basically, if we cannot yet recognize for ourselves in a concrete way that everything is already perfect and perfectly enlightened, if we

Fruit Seven

still feel that samsara is bad and nirvana is good, then we are still in the realm of dualistic suffering. There is no fundamental difference, on an absolute level, between samsara and nirvana.

The equality of all phenomena is not something you can grok with your ordinary mind, your ethics, your smart intellect, or even your science. It may not have much bearing on your day-to-day life until you experience it directly for yourself through sadhana or other means. Even then, you have to become established in that experience. Until that time, we all should try to relate to dualistic experience using our practice and should follow our tradition's precepts and guidelines.

When we directly experience the equality of all phenomena, we have the firsthand understanding that when someone gets born or dies, or a war happens, or peace happens, all of these are aspects of the infinite expressivity of wisdom and its energy. This incredible ornamental display or glamour is the Supreme Self accomplishing its nature. We can enjoy the whole palette of emotions. We can live rich, participatory lives. We can go out and protest inequities if we so choose, and we can try to make things better out of natural compassion. However, we will cease to be caught in a prison of urgency and despair. We can participate in life as we choose, yet being established in the equality of all phenomena, we know fundamentally that nothing is wrong, and that there is only goodness here. There is a primordial goodness that supersedes relative good and evil, nirvana and samsara.

When we get upset about the destructive aspects of life, we are getting upset because of stuff happening that we don't like, or feel is wrong. For instance, when somebody dies, we often feel something unfair or tragic has occurred. But from an absolute perspective, no person has ever been born. No one has ever lived a life as an independent being, and nothing has ever died. What has actually happened is that a real appearing of wisdom and energy has arisen along with a bunch of other forms, and they're enacting a drama.

Think of it this way: when a wave subsides back into the ocean, we don't feel that is a tragedy. We understand that the ocean has just changed form. Nothing independent was ever created, and nothing has died. So it's not that literally nothing has happened, it just hasn't happened in the way that we think it has happened. Our mistake is not that we experience all of these individual phenomena; our mistake is thinking that they exist independently on the most fundamental level.

When we are not mistaking the relative for the absolute, and when we are established in the equality of all phenomena, we can enjoy all of the different emotions that we have here and all of the different circumstances. We can experience pain and joy and loss and gain and appreciate all of them in a way that we didn't before. This is real equanimity, not blandness or lack of emotion.

When we have this foundation in the equality of all phenomena, then we are free to experience more and express ourselves more. We start to appreciate life and other people on a profound and vast scale. We can see that other people are the expressions of this reality and have equal value as that. Instead of being all involved in judging people, or defending ourselves against people, or aggressing against people, or manipulating people, we can simply appreciate how others are showing up.

Fruit Seven

FRUIT EIGHT

Discovering ananda — aesthetic delight in the creation

Do you remember the portrayals of East Germany and the Soviet Union in movies and TV shows about the Cold War period? How did filmmakers brand these countries as totalitarian? Everything was gray! Citizens wore gray or brown shapeless, boring clothes. The buildings were gray and anonymous and decrepit. The food was bland and colorless. Much of the critique of totalitarianism was conveyed through aesthetics. The State had no appreciation for beauty. You weren't allowed to read certain books or enjoy certain music. The buildings weren't architecturally interesting. You weren't allowed to express yourself politically, of course, but deeply embedded in these versions of totalitarianism was the lack of freedom to express yourself aesthetically.[32]

When we take a step back, it's surprising that the lack of creative, aesthetic freedom plays such a big role in our feelings about and portrayals of totalitarianism. What does this tell us about our concept of freedom? And even more, what does it tell us about our longing for freedom? When we long for freedom, what are we actually longing for? Is the longing for freedom of creative expression, or freedom of self-expression in the forefront? It's interesting to consider that unfreedom might, when all of the layers are peeled back, mean lack of freedom to express oneself creatively. Think about this: if you had to choose, would you rather live as you are now, out in the world, but lacking the freedom to express yourself, or would you choose to be imprisoned physically, but with the freedom to write and dance and sing and speak freely and generally express yourself as you wish?

Think about when you wake up in the morning. As you wake up, you may enjoy the texture of your sheets. Hopefully, as you open your eyes, you feel glad because you like the colors and textures and arrangement of items in your bedroom. You choose your clothing not just in a utilitarian way, but also according to the colors and textures and shapes that please you. And then maybe you eat a tasty breakfast, one that also pleases you visually and appeals to your other senses.

During the day, you engage in many conversations. Most of these conversations include some element of story-telling about yourself, others, and various circumstances. We can even include gossip here. Perhaps you enjoy expressing yourself in a certain way, or you indulge in wordplay, or you notice and enjoy others doing the same. More stories inhabit your day from Facebook or YouTube or the news. Think about how reporters speak of their work in terms of "news stories' and "getting the story." Think about how much dramatic flair goes into supposedly reporting simply what happens. Some would even say that there is more flair than substance in the reporting of the so-called news. As you go along in your day, you enjoy the images and colors on your computer screen. And then at night, maybe you're going to watch TV or go to the movies, or tell the story of your day to your loved ones, or read stories to your children.

If you step back and take a wider view of the situation, your life is almost entirely spent making aesthetic choices, enjoying aesthetic productions, telling stories, and hearing stories. Even if you think of yourself as the most uncreative person, your day is filled with all kinds of aesthetic choices and enjoyments that are aesthetic on some level. Isn't that interesting?

Now imagine that you live on a planet where nobody cares about aesthetic experience. This imagined world has no art, no music, no painting, no novels, no dance, no movies, no theater. No one really cares how they dress. No one enjoys stories. No one cares what words they use. Food is prepared without regard for aesthetic considerations. When you compare this hypothetical life to how we live, you can see how extreme we are in structuring everything around aesthetic enjoyment.

When David Bowie died, it amazed me how people and institutions from around the world—even very conservative institutions and governments—celebrated his life. Church bells played his songs, and officials in town halls made speeches about him. A space station crew played Space Oddity while they circled the earth. Bowie cut across so many cultures and strata of society. He was unconventional, but he had a magical quality that moved many different kinds of people.

The word that keeps coming to me when I contemplate this "Bowie effect" is the Buddhist term, *sambhogakaya*. Sambhogakaya means the body of enjoyment. Sambhogakaya relates to magical, jewel-like appearings such as those in dazzling, visionary dreams; the subtle forms of mandalas; and the play of *dakinis*, Buddhas, and deities. It is a mode of reality in which complex, colorful, effervescent forms can arise and easily transform. Dakinis are called sky dancers, meaning that they can create beauty and art and dance in a subtle way with just energy and color, just light and energy.

When I was a little kid, I used to have an incredible ability to visualize. I would lie on my bed and project pictures onto the wall in front of me. The pictures were as clear as if I was literally watching a movie. I would project these images for hours on end. It was so entertaining. That's a kind of sambhogakaya experience.

Bowie reminded us of our sambhogakaya power through the creative freedom that he displayed, his lightness and playfulness, and also kindness. He was a very kind person, a very gentle person despite all his wildness. He evoked that longing to be more free to create and express ourselves; to be elegant and play with our way of showing up in the world.

Our more limited aesthetic enjoyment is actually a direct reflection of ananda, the aesthetic delight inherent in the creation. Ananda is usually translated as bliss. Bliss is a misleading translation that has given rise to a lot of new age fantasy. Our ordinary-mind idea of bliss is an individual, bubbly, happy feeling, or some permutation of that. But this doesn't really have much to do with ananda. Ananda is beyond any ordinary idea of bliss. Ananda really means bliss plus clarity, and more specifically aesthetic delight, or delighting in one's own creative expressions. You could call it divine appreciation.

When you write a poem, you read it over and over again. When you paint a painting, you step back and enjoy it. A large part of the magic of this situation is that you have started with only an idea or inspiration or image coming from within you. Now it is outside of you, and you can contemplate, not just the creative production, but your own nature made manifest. When you are enjoying and feeling wonder at your own creations, you are being a lot like God.

All manifest life is a projection of the Supreme Self. Ananda truly means the feeling-perceiving-amazed state of the Supreme as it delights in continously contemplating the creation as a reflection of its own nature. Lalleshwari, the 14th century Kashmiri yogini said that, "The experience of God is continuous amazement."[33] This is a direct reflection of the state of God. Now let's remember the principle of "as above so below." We are made of and by unconditioned consciousness and energy. Nothing that's happening here can be radically different or completely divorced from that enlightened essence nature. It's just not possible. If you were a sculptor, you could not make a sculpture that was completely non-expressive of you. It would not be possible.

As this alive aware reality contemplates its own nature through its creative productions, we are also, in our own way, with all our limitations, attempting to do this and experience a kind of everyday ananda. We are experiencing an echo of ananda when we put on the clothes that we enjoy, when we enjoy a sunset, when we are amazed at the special effects in a movie, and when we enjoy the words that someone is speaking, or that we're speaking.

The capacities of our senses, including our minds, are rather stepped down from the full-on experience of enlightened essence nature. When we do sadhana, we are opening the gates of our senses. We are pouring our little senses into God's *maha*, or great, senses. We are reintegrating our mind and all of our other senses back into that aware, alive reality. Along the way, our aesthetic capacity gains strength, refinement, clarity, subtlety, and precision. I can tell you about this from personal experience. We recognize the experience of having two physical eyes, and some of us are comfortable talking about a third eye. But there are actually five eyes. Or maybe more. Who knows? But I know about five eyes.

When I started having openings of the fourth and fifth eyes, vision was developing in a particular sequence from the gross physical eyes to the subtler fifth eye. I searched on the Internet to see if there were any descriptions of this. I did find some Buddhist teachings on the five eyes. I also found articles about a shadowy international governmental organization called The Five Eyes! In any case, the fifth eye is when you are seeing with seeing. In other words, you no longer need the pretense of physical eyes to engage with this reality's immanent capacity for sight. Fifth-eye vision is clearer and more pristine than anything you can see with physical eyes. It blazes with color and light more intensely than any computer screen. It is actual perfect vision, beyond time and space. It is beautiful, but also impossible to sustain, at least for me.

Fruit Eight

The clarity of perception of God is exponentially greater than our ordinary clarity. If in one moment we were suddenly to be totally enlightened, we would be completely freaked out by the level of perception and the level of sensation and the level of clarity. It would be too much for us to bear. However, in the course of doing spiritual practice, we may notice that colors gradually look more saturated or clearer, or that we're seeing or hearing or tasting or smelling more clearly. Sometimes our senses can feel a little bit too sharp. This occurs as we wake up more. We have to recalibrate.

Our ability to appreciate the aesthetic aspect of everything also increases. Even as we encounter a painful or negative situation, we are simultaneously aware of the beauty of it and the intelligence that infuses it. We are more attuned to qualities, colors, and sensations, and also subtle energetic qualities. In the process of entering more fully into this kind of multi-dimensional perception and feeling, our emotional habit patterns loosen their grip on us. This just progresses as we go along.

One time I had a dream in which Anandamayi Ma gave me a blessing. At the end, I was walking down a staircase. I was singing Durga's name, and I was dancing down these steps. My entire being was an expression of the delight and the musicality of reality. These kinds of transmissions stay with you. You learn about your own nature, and you also get a glimpse of where you're going. You have a beacon. This dream taught me about the sensation of clarity, and not just about seeing things clearly. There's a sensation of clarity that's really hard to describe, but I guess it has to do with being aware of everything at once. You're not blocking anything out. You are totally immersed in every aspect of experience. Every cell in your body is perceiving. Usually we're walking around with blinders on all of our senses.

I keep harping on clarity because I think we forget about that. Clarity of understanding, clarity of View, clarity of perception, clarity of sensation. All of these things are possible and inevitable if we keep practicing.

FRUIT NINE

Taking refuge only in the natural state

Fruit Nine

Samsara is characterized by labor. We labor to cobble together a sense of self. We labor to defend ourselves. We compete and labor to succeed. When we take refuge in the natural state, we stop struggling. To take refuge means to come to a state of rest. We stop trying to bend the will of the world to our own will. We enter into a relationship of objectless reciprocity and responsivity to life. We are listening, following, cooperating with, adapting to, and enjoying what is, rather than struggling our way through and against circumstances.

During the basic Buddhist initiation, a student takes refuge in Buddha, Dharma, and Sangha (in the Guru, in the teachings, and in the community of like-minded people). Although most beginning students relate only to the individual, concrete, obvious manifestations of these three refuges, each of these refuges is a living symbol of the natural, enlightened state. This is the ultimate and only refuge, the only real ashram.

Anandamayi Ma said: "This body does not build ashrams. There is one all pervading and all transcendent ashram - where whatever you say [see] is there…Really the entire world is just an ashram of this body. Where is the second? Ashram means a place where there is no labor."[34]

Shram means fatigue, exhaustion, and depleting exertion or labor. *Ashram* means without those qualities. Ma is saying that all manifest life, the entire world, is an ashram *if we are serving and are devoted to the ultimate: our real enlightened nature.* Suffering is not inherent in the world; we suffer because of our limitations. We can build a structure in which to relax and take refuge, such as an ashram, or a spa or even an ordinary house. Many of us try to take refuge in an ordinary living space. But then we will be settling for what is incomplete and temporary. Until we recognize and take refuge in the all-pervading ashram—enlightened essence nature—we will suffer.

When we feel separate and subject to various compulsive patterns of body, energy, and mind, then we will inevitably feel something is wrong, or missing. We experience craving and longing. We seek fulfillment, contentment, and relief from the burden of the self. But the more ignorant we are, the more we seek those things in a way that perpetuates our habit patterns. We seek refuge in what is familiar, conventional, pleasant, and most importantly, what is ephemeral.

We humans attempt to take refuge in all sorts of things. We take refuge in our familiar emotional habit patterns of sadness, anger, criticism, and jealousy. We take refuge in pleasure and in comfort. We take refuge in relationships and in our possessions. We take refuge in our jobs or whatever we think it is that is going to resolve that feeling of lack and give us some feeling of contentment or fulfillment or relief. Yet when we try to seek refuge in impermanence—inevitably our refuge will go away, and we will no longer feel a sense of respite or relief. There is no end to sorrow, want, and longing.

Fruit Nine

In the U.S., we have this weird phenomenon that has emerged from our psychologization of everything. People actually try to take refuge in feeling badly about themselves. Unfortunately, feeling badly about yourself has become a kind of social currency. We connect with other people by talking about how badly we feel about ourselves, and how hard things are for us. We've been trained to do that. It's not a good training.

Worrying is also an unreliable refuge. In fact, worry is a completely failed strategy that tries to freeze the inexorable flow of circumstance. When we worry about stuff, we go around and around, over and over again. Nothing ever gets resolved. We freeze in this pattern. We are ultimately trying to stop time, to stop death. Remember a time when you were really worried about something, and you stopped thinking about it for a moment because some external activity distracted you. Then, when that activity was complete, you felt scared because you weren't worrying about that thing for a few moments. You feel as if you are in freefall when you're not hanging onto worrying. But being in that freefall is the best remedy. It is an encounter with emptiness. So try not to take refuge in worrying about yourself. Use your practice to become acclimatized to the sensation of emptiness or openness. See how it goes!

This wise, aware reality speaks to us in the form of our hunger for the ultimate, for supreme connection and continuity. It never stops speaking until we reach the goal. This is natural law. Suppose you buy the perfect house, the one you've always wanted. Immediately after the sale goes through, you experience buyer's remorse. You find many things wrong and experience a familiar, gnawing sense of lack. Or maybe you're in what you think is the perfect relationship. But you still have this terrible sense of separation shadowing your happiness. If your partner goes on a business trip, or spends "too much" time with a friend, or expresses doubts about being with you, suddenly your happiness vanishes, and the feeling of panic and wanting appears again. Our own enlightened essence nature is telling us that we should keep on until we discover who we really are and can take refuge in that. Impermanence causes discontent. Desire for fulfillment causes us to seek the eternal. Combined, discontent and desire eventually lead us home.

After many disappointments, and after opportunity has arisen for us to rediscover living presence, the desire to seek refuge in what is temporary subsides, and the desire to seek refuge in unconditioned essence nature intensifies. The capacity to identify with living presence increases, and the deadly seriousness with which we take our ordinary pursuits decreases. The desperation with which we cling to the elements of impermanence wanes, and the desperation with which we seek to identify with living presence waxes. Anandamayi Ma was asked, "What is the means of entering the tide?" She answered, "To ask this question with desperate eagerness."[35]

The energy of your compulsions and limited desires is redirected by the force of daily sadhana. At some point, you begin to desperately desire to discover who you really are, and that desire fuels your practice further. At a later phase, you recognize essence nature everywhere. You have developed the capacity to remember presence, to relate to wisdom, more unbrokenly. One word for lack of realization is "forgetting." Realizing is "remembering." When we remember most of the time, we are approaching a condition of *akhanda sadhana*, or continuous sadhana. We can remember the aware livingness of everything and integrate with that rather than with limitations.

For a long time after you have recognized living presence, that recognition comes and goes. You can't hold onto it because your karmic patterns have too much momentum. They keep dragging you away from the recognition of your real nature and back into ordinary perceptions and habits of body, energy, and mind. But there also comes a time when your awareness of the Supreme never goes away. It waxes and wanes. It won't be complete, but it never goes away entirely.

At that point, you can enjoy ordinary life a lot more because you no longer worry about it. You can feel much more forgiving about your own fixations. You already have seen for yourself that everything is coming from the same source and is made of the same source. So why worry? You are not so reactive to what other people say and do because other people aren't so "other" anymore, and you can perceive directly the wisdom in every circumstance. You lose the strong sense of discontinuity between you and other people. Your life unfolds normally, but it no longer feels as if anything much is at stake. Or at least you host your foibles and fixations with a healthy dose of humor and self-irony.

Eventually, as Ma says, "Sustained effort ends in effortless being."[36] Inside and outside cease to be meaningful on anything but a functional level. You no longer feel separate from others, or from life. You recognize that this timeless, living presence is your own nature. You can just relax. When that happens, your fear of dying is greatly reduced. Your fear of difficulties and loss vanish. You experience more curiosity about the world. You express yourself more freely and are free to play with circumstance. Your life becomes more like improvisational music.

Waking up is about enlarging your View. If your View is really big, if you are integrating with presence, a fender bender is just a tiny little thing in a huge landscape. If there is no other, if there is one continuous living awareness, then there is no one here to hurt anybody else, no one here to leave anybody else, no one here to disappoint anybody else, nothing to lose, nothing to really gain. You can play freely in the field of duality, engaging with the appearings of this creative, self-aware wisdom.

More profoundly, you now naturally desire to give what you have to give. Generosity is a fountain of living light at the heart of creation. The creation itself, the existence of worlds, is the supreme generosity. Having opened your heart and recognized its identity with the heart of the divine, you want to be here giving and giving throughout your natural lifetime.

Fruit Nine

The good news is that if you practice a lot and are sincere, you don't have to wait until you're enlightened to experience more freedom of expression and to beautifully embody many wisdom virtues. You don't have to wait to express natural generosity and to experience greater spontaneity, clarity, and joy. Just do your practice every day. Try your best to be in the state of your practice at all times, integrating with presence and developing your clarity. Wisdom takes care of the rest.

ENDNOTES

1. Longchenpa, "Longchenpa on Obstacles," trans. Erik Tsiknopoulos. Retrieved January 17, 2017, from https://buddha-nature.com/2016/12/12/longchenpa-on-obstacles/.

2. An Internet search on keywords "Buddhism" or "Zen" and "obstacles" will reveal any number of sources.

3. I recommend *The Mahabharata: a Modern Rendering* by Ramesh Menon.

4. Freud's method is demonstrated in any of the numerous published collections of his case studies.

5. Gurupriya Ananda Giri, *Sri Sri Anandamayi*, trans. Tara Kini (Calcutta: Shree Shree Anandamayee Charitable Society, 1986), 160-1.

6. Quoted in Sogyal, Patrick Gaffney, and Andrew Harvey, *The Tibetan Book of Living and Dying*, (San Francisco, Calif.: HarperSanFrancisco, 2002), 170.

7. See Mother Teresa and Brian Kolodiejchuk, *Mother Teresa: Come Be My Light: The Private Writings of the Saint of Calcutta,*

(Crown Publishing Group, 2007).

8. Ram Kumar Rai, *Kulārnava Tantra*, (Varanasi: Prachya Prakashan, 1983), 17-21.

9. Anandamayi Ma, "Mātri Satsang in Vrindaban," *Ananda Varta* 23, NO. 1 (1976): 4.

10. Richard Lannoy, *Anandamayi: Her Life and Wisdom*, (Rockport, MA: Element, 1996), 73.

11. Thich Nhat Hanh, *The Heart of the Buddha's Teaching: Transforming Suffering into Peace, Joy and Liberation: The Four Noble Truths, the Noble Eightfold Path, and Other Basic Buddhist Teachings*, (New York: Broadway Books, 1999), 221-248.

12. Chögyam Trungpa and Carolyn Rose Gimian, *Shambhala: The Sacred Path of the Warrior*, (Boulder, Colo.: Shambhala, 1984), 13-17.

13. Liu Ming, *Changing Zhouyi: The Heart of the Yijing*, (Oakland, CA: Da Yuan Circle, 2005).

14. Swami Bhagavatananda Giri, "Matri Satsang in Solan," *Ananda Varta* 20, NO. 2 (1973): 86.

15. Anandamayi Ma, *Ma in Her Words*, privately circulated manuscript: 97.

16. Swami Lakshmanjoo, *Vijñana Bhairava Tantra: The Practice of Centering Awareness*, trans. Bettina Bäumer (Varanasi: Indica, 2002), 1-15.

17. Anandamayi Ma, "Matri Vani," *Ma Anandamayee Amrit Varta* 2, NO. 1 (1998): 2.

18. Padmasambhava, *Advice from the Lotus-Born: A Collection of Padmasambhava's Advice to the Dakini Yeshe Tsogyal and Other Close Disciples*, trans. Erik Pema Kunsang (Hong Kong: Rangjung Yeshe Publications, 2004), 12.

19. Moti Lal Pandit, *The Trika Saivism of Kashmir*, (New Delhi: Munshiram Monoharlal Publishers Pvt. Ltd., 2003), 89.

20. Paul Eduardo Muller-Ortega, *The Triadic Heart of Śiva: Kaula*

Tantricism of Abhinavagupta in the Non-Dual Shaivism of Kashmir, (Albany, NY: SUNY P, 1989), 138-9.

21. See, for instance, Hugh B. Urban, *Songs of Ecstasy: Tantric and Devotional Songs from Colonial Bengal,* (Oxford: Oxford University Press, 2001).

22. See, for instance, Chan Master Sheng Yen, *There Is No Suffering: A Commentary on the Heart Sutra,* (Elmhurst, N.Y.: Dharma Drum Publications, 2001).

23. Mark Elliot, Director, *The Lion's Roar*, Crestone Films, 1985. This documentary includes the story of the death of the 16th Karmapa in the United States.

24. See Endnote #14 above.

25. John of the Cross, *Dark Night of the Soul*, trans. E. Allison Peers (New York: Image Books, Doubleday, 1990).

26. See Endnote #13 above.

27. See Endnote #21 above.

28. Christina Lundberg, Director, *For the Benefit of All Beings: The Extraordinary Life of His Eminence Garchen Triptrul Rinpoche,* Garuda Sky Productions, 2008. This documentary tells the story of the life of Garchen Rinpoche and includes his testimony regarding the twenty years he was incarcerated in a Chinese labor camp.

29. Anandamayi Ma, "Matri Vani," *Ananda Varta* 11, NO. 1 (1963): 4.

30. Anandamayi Ma, *Words of Sri Anandamayi Ma*, trans. Atmananda (Hardwar: Shree Shree Anandamayee Sangha Kankhal, 2008), 135-140.

31. Ibid., 93-7.

32. The 1996 British film, *Funeral in Berlin*, is a good example.

33. Coleman Barks, *Naked Song: Lalla*, trans. Coleman Barks (Athens, GA: Maypop Books, 1992), 50.

34. Anandamayi Ma, *Ma in Her Words*: 19.

35. Lannoy, 107.

36. Anandamayi Ma, *Words of Sri Anandamayi Ma*, 64.

Endnotes

STUDY GUIDE

My students came to me and said that they would like to offer a suggestion to readers of this book. In our community, students dedicate each month to exploring and discussing a single precept, or guideline for dharmic living. They do this on a communications platform called Slack. They have enjoyed this practice and suggest that readers of this book may want to form their own discussion-practice groups with friends on or offline. You could choose one poison, medicine, or fruit to explore each month in discussion with others and in your own life. Some suggestions for free discussion platforms are Slack, HipChat, Facebook groups, GoodReads, and LibraryThing. Feel free to copy and share this list of the nine poisons, nine medicines, and nine fruits.

Nine Poisons

1. Self-concern at the expense of others
2. Self-neglect at the expense of the capacity to realize
3. Over-reliance on individualistic will
4. Mistaking thinking about life for direct experience

5. Feeling there is a fundamental difference between success and failure
6. Running after pleasure
7. Avoiding pain and fear
8. Mistaking good and bad and right and wrong for absolutes
9. Mistaking temporary appeasements for the goal

Nine Medicines

1. Being forced to recognize the intrinsic value of others
2. Feeling horror at the arising and slipping away of opportunity
3. Feeling overwhelmed by circumstances and being forced to ask for help
4. Feeling the loneliness that comes from maintaining a conceptual relationship to life
5. Feeling exhausted by your own striving
6. Finding your usual pleasures to be hollow and boring
7. Recognizing the wisdom in pain and fear
8. Realizing that waking life is like a painting, a drama, or a dream
9. Recognizing that you are always dissatisfied in the end

Nine Fruits

1. Delighting in expressing kindness
2. Attending courageously and devotedly to the conditions that make it possible to realize
3. Delighting in the play of alliance
4. Delighting in the play of continuous conversation
5. Delighting in skillfully adapting to the play of circumstance
6. Tasting the sweetness of everything
7. Recognizing the equality of all phenomena
8. Discovering ananda—aesthetic delight in the creation
9. Taking refuge only in the natural state

ACKNOWLEDGMENTS

Thanks to my teachers and gratitude for living in a Reality that causes teachers and teachings to appear. Thanks to my editors Matridarshana Lamb and Dorothy Drennen. Thanks to Gangotri Ferris, Ariel Singer, and Ambika Beber. Thanks to all of the students who recorded these teachings, preserved them, and transcribed them.